EARLY CHILDHOOD EDUCATION SERIES

Leslie R. Williams, Editor

ADVISORY BOARD: Barbara T. Bowman, Harriet K. Cuffaro, Stephanie Feeney, Doris Pronin Fromberg, Celia Genishi, Stacie G. Goffin, Dominic F. Gullo, Alice Sterling Honig, Elizabeth Jones, Gwen Morgan

(continued)

HOW TO WORK
WITH STANDARDS

in the

Early Childhood Classroom

Carol Seefeldt

Teachers College, Columbia University
New York and London

KH

Published by Teachers College Press, 1234 Amsterdam Avenue, New York, NY 10027

Library of Congress Cataloging-in-Publication Data

Seefeldt, Carol.
    How to work with standards in the early childhood classroom / Carol Seefeldt.
      p. cm. — (Early childhood education series)
    Includes bibliographical references and index.
    ISBN 0-8077-4587-1 (pbk.)
    1. Early childhood education—Curricula—United States. 2. Early childhood education—Standards—United States.
  3. Curriculum planning—United States. I. Title. II. Early childhood education series (Teachers College Press)

LB1139.4.S44 2005
372.21 22   2004063792

ISBN 0-8077-4587-1 (paper)

Printed on acid-free paper

Manufactured in the United States of America

12 11 10 09 08 07 06 05   8 7 6 5 4 3 2 1

9/5/06

To Dr. Alice Galper,
a dedicated friend and treasured colleague.

Contents

Preface

There is no doubt that today's early childhood educator will be asked to implement standards and assess children's learning. It is essential that preservice and in-service teachers become knowledgeable of standards and how to work with them.

This book has been designed as a resource for early childhood educators as they grapple with a plethora of issues, questions, philosophies, and the practicalities of working with standards of early learning for children in preschool through kindergarten and Grades 1–3. It not only offers teachers a base of historical knowledge and philosophical understanding of the standards movement in general, but also provides practical strategies for the implementation and assessment of standards of learning for young children in the early childhood classroom.

With the knowledge and understanding gained from this book, teachers will be able to

1. Effectively judge and select standards
2. Design appropriate ways of using and implementing standards
3. Develop appropriate assessment strategies

Currently, the field of early education is overwhelmed with standards. While standards delineating what elementary and secondary students should know and be able to do by a given grade have been available since the late 1980s, the reality of standards is just now making inroads in early education. About 30 state departments of education or early learning programs provide standards for learning for children between the ages of birth and 5 (Kagan, Scott-Little, & Frelow, 2003). Other state offices for children, local school systems, and state agencies are in the process of instituting standards of learning for children during the early years.

ORGANIZATION OF THE BOOK

How to Work with Standards in the Early Childhood Classroom is divided into three parts. Part I reviews the history of standards within the context of school reform (Chapter 1) and describes the standards in the field of early education for children in preschool through kindergarten and the primary grades (Chapter 2). Although the term *standard* has multiple meanings, in this era of accountability the term is most often associated with the quality of education. The standards movement is a part of the drive to provide quality educational experiences for all students in the United States. The quality of what students learn, the quality of the systems delivering education, the quality of teachers and their preparation, and the quality of curriculum content and its assessment are intended to be improved through the provision of standards.

Part II presents the issues surrounding evaluating and selecting standards. Chapters 3 and 4 offer teachers realistic guides for selecting standards and working with benchmarks. While practical in nature, these chapters are grounded in research and theory. The philosophy of constructivism permeates this part because I believe that children are active learners who learn through their own mental, physical, and social activity. It is from knowledge of how children learn, grow, and develop that standards can be judged and implemented.

Part III is based on the premise that standards of learning can integrate the total curriculum. Standards from each of the separate content areas—mathematics, language and literacy, the arts, sciences, and social studies—advocate two kinds of integration: The first is integration within the particular subject matter, and the second is integrating each separate subject matter throughout the entire curriculum. Standards from each of the separate subject matter disciplines are firmly grounded on the belief that students are to think, create, and solve problems. In Chapter 5, I show how the common threads of problem solving, thinking, and creating that are found throughout each set of standards unite the separate subject disciplines into an integrated whole. In Chapters 6–10, I demonstrate how to work with standards in the separate subject areas. Ideas for including all children who present themselves at the classroom door and for assessing learning are found throughout the chapters. At the end of each chapter in Part III is a description of a continuing investigation of the children's world. This project, Children Study Their Play Yard, illustrates how thematic, standards-based, problem-solving learning can integrate the total curriculum.

Acknowledgments

Once again I acknowledge the expertise and guidance of Susan Liddicoat, who initiated this book. Her sensitive and caring competence guided its development.

The children and faculty of the Center for Young Children, University of Maryland, College Park, are acknowledged. Work from their integrated investigations of their world illustrate *How to Work with Standards*. Fran Favretto and Francince Sacchetti are to be commended for grounding the curriculum of the Center for Young Children on children's firsthand study of their world and standards of learning. Special recognition is given to Jennifer Smallwood and Stefanie Adamson who gave permission to photograph children in their classroom. I sincerely appreciate the generosity of the families who gave their permission to have their children photographed.

PART I

UNDERSTANDING STANDARDS

CHAPTER 1

The Development of Standards

The term *standard* has multiple meanings. Common to all is the idea that a standard is something of recognized value or excellence, an agreed-on model that can be used as a basis of comparison. We all use standards daily. Any time we weigh or measure something, we are using a standard. The money we use is based on a standard. Even the language we use is determined by the agreed-on, valued, or preferred way of using and pronouncing words.

Now the term *standard* is being applied to the field of education, including early childhood education. The idea is that just as we measure a pound of bananas expecting to receive the same amount each time we buy a pound, so should we expect all children at the same level of schooling to receive the same amount and quality of educational experiences. In addition, academic standards declare what every student should know and be able to do in core academic content areas. Academic standards also define how students are to demonstrate their knowledge and skills.

Driven by the belief that every child in the United States should receive an agreed-on standard of educational experiences, the term *academic standards* can apply to the quality of the systems delivering education, the quality of teachers and their preparation, and the quality of curriculum content and its assessment. The premise of academic standards is that by implementing standards for systems, teachers, and the curriculum, the quality of educational experiences all children receive will be improved (National Research Council [NRC] 2001b; Wraga & Hiebowitsh, 2003).

The goals of this chapter are to

- Present the history leading to the development of national standards
- Discuss the rational for today's standards

STANDARDS—THEIR HISTORY

Much is expected of public education in the United States. With the goal of preparing the young to become productive members of a democratic society, public education is held responsible, not just for the successes of our society, but for its failures as well.

Historically, whenever social or economic forces threatened the status quo, public education received the blame and responsibility (Tanner & Tanner, 1990). The curriculum—what was taught in schools and what children learned—was examined and determined to be lacking throughout the history of the United States. Education was said to be "in crisis" before and after the Revolutionary War, before and after the Great Depression of the 1930s, during the Second World War, and during and after the civil rights movement through to today.

Social and Economic Forces

Now, however, social and economic forces have converged in ways that place increasing pressure on what is being taught in the public schools. Public schools are called "broken." Citizens decry the state of public education, especially in large cities. Large city school systems are in financial and administrative crisis. Superintendents and boards of education in large cities disagree. Parents and community groups rally in support of public education, but improvement seems difficult to achieve and maintain.

Financially unstable and without continuity of administration, schools in inner cities differ from those in more affluent areas of the nation creating two levels of school systems in our nation. Children living in poverty fail to achieve in our ill-equipped inner-city schools. Without enough teachers, books, computers, and other necessary materials of schooling, children are unable to thrive academically. On the other hand, children schooled in wealthier areas typically are taught by well-prepared teachers in beautifully equipped buildings with a wealth of resources available for their learning.

Adding to the nation's concerns for the improvement of schools, the small, but highly influential and vocal, Far Right, calls for the complete abolishment of public education (Agape Press, 2004). These citizens are concerned that their children are learning values that contradict their own, and take the stance that even reforms will not make public education acceptable. Thus this group withdraws their children from public education, choosing to school their children at home or in a religious school (Barbour & Barbour, 1997). To further their stated goal of eliminating public education, the Far Right supports school vouchers, federal monies for religious schools, federal funding for faith-based programs, and charter schools.

Picking up on the rhetoric of the conservative groups, others also call for total school reform. They cite selected international studies of student achievement, particularly the International Mathematics and Science Study (Martin & Kelly, 1998), which show that children in the United States achieve lower than those in 14 other nations including Korea, Hong Kong SAR, and Japan.

Regardless of their motives, those calling for school reform want American children to have the best schooling possible. With standards in place for systems and programs, for teacher preparation, and for the curriculum, people are more likely to believe that the best educational experience can be provided for every child in the nation.

The Beginnings

The pervasive dissatisfaction with public education can be traced back to 1957 when Sputnik I, the artificial satellite launched by Russia, began circling the earth. Then, as now, schools were called upon to remedy society's concerns. Since Russia beat the United States into space, the conclusion was that students in the United States were not being educated properly to lead the world in scientific progress.

Accusations were biting. The school curriculum was labeled as lacking in the academics, as well as in quality, discipline, and rigor (Tanner & Tanner, 1990). Deweyian philosophy, problem solving and discovery learning, and other child-centered approaches that had their roots in the 1930s and 1940s, came to a halt even before they were fully implemented, especially in the secondary schools. New visions of curriculum full of rigor and intellectual challenge were advanced by philosophers, scientists, and educators. Strong pressures to raise standards and enrollments in the "rigorous" subjects—science, mathematics, and foreign languages—took place. During the Sputnik period, high school graduations increased, and achievement scores on all kinds of tests showed increases (Ravitch, 1995a).

Nevertheless, the Sputnik era ended quickly as social upheavals and political movements led to radical school innovations. The angst over Vietnam and the civil rights movement of the 1960s led to calls for additional curriculum reforms. The "new math"—teaching math for meaning—open enrollment in colleges and universities, freedom to choose courses, and other reforms given the rubric of "open education" were implemented.

Jerome Bruner (1966) advocated a new theory of instruction. Based on the idea that the curriculum was "an effort to assist or to shape growth" (p. 1), Bruner proposed that meaningful curriculum should teach the young to think for themselves and take part in the process of knowledge getting, and declared that "knowing is a process, not a product" (p. 72).

The work of Jean Piaget (1969), just becoming known in the United States, was used to support meaningful, experiential learning. Piaget advanced the hypothesis that children construct their own knowledge. Anything told to children was secondhand knowledge.

Bruner thought of the curriculum as a process, not a product.

Real learning, according to Piagetian theories, required mental activity: Children had to think about, reflect on, and process their firsthand experiences with their physical world and with other children and adults.

Coupled with the new curriculum of the 1960s and 1970s were declining SAT scores. The decline in SAT scores began in 1963 and continued to decline through the 1970s. Concerned about the low achievement of high school students President Carter in 1977 called for a commission to study the curriculum. The commission found that American students were taking fewer mathematics and science courses and virtually no foreign language courses (Ravitch, 1995a).

A Call for Standards

The lower achievement of high school and college students did not go unnoticed. The College Board speculated that television and changes in the family, as well as the disruptive events of the Watergate scandal and the horrors of the war in Vietnam were to blame. Others blamed the declining test scores on the heritage of the 1960s, including the influence of the theories of Piaget, Bruner, and the resurgence of Dewey's philosophy (Ravitch, 1995a).

No report or event, however, was as influential in leading to school reform as the publication of *A Nation at Risk* in 1983. Prepared by the National Commission on Excellence in Education at the request of the Secretary of Education, *A Nation at Risk* characterized the American educational system as "being eroded" by a tide of mediocrity that "threatens our very future as a nation" (p. 5).

A Nation at Risk received a great deal of attention. Legislators used the premise of the report to increase their rhetoric on the need for school reform. The Far Right used it to promote their goal of abolishing public education. The press and public alike lavished attention on the report (Ravitch, 1995a). A variety of federal and state legislation designed to improve the quality of education students receive, and hence student achievement, was passed. Included in this legislation were specific goals for student learning.

Reflecting concern for the need to improve public education, the nation's governors convened at the Education Summit in Charlottesville, Virginia, in 1989. To meet the challenges of a rapidly changing world, new levels of achievement were called for, beginning with higher expectations for America's educational system.

Concluding the meeting, the governors established six broad goals for education that were to be achieved by the year 2000. Two additional goals were added later. The first goal relates directly to early childhood education:

Goal 1: All children in America will start school ready to learn. The objectives for this goal are that (1) all children would have access to high-quality appropriate preschool programs; (2) all parents will be their child's first teacher and devote time each day to their children's education; (3) children will receive the nutrition, health care, and physical activity required for them to arrive at school with healthy minds and bodies.

The goals directed toward elementary and secondary education are as follows:

Goal 2: School completion. By the year 2000 high school graduation will increase to at least 90 percent.

Goal 3: Student achievement and citizenship. By the year 2000 all students will leave Grades 4, 8, and 12 having demonstrated competency over challenging subject matter including English, mathematics, sciences, foreign languages, civics and government, economics, the arts, history, and geography.

Goal 4: Teacher education and professional development. By the year 2000 the nation's teachers will have access to the continued improvement of their professional skills.

Goal 5: Mathematics and science. By the year 2000, United States students will be first in the world in mathematics and science achievement.

Goal 6: Adult literacy and lifelong learning. By the year 2000 every adult American will be literate and will possess the knowledge and skills necessary to compete in a global economy and exercise the rights and responsibilities of citizenship.

Goal 7: Safe, disciplined, and alcohol- and drug-free schools. Every school in the United States will be free of drugs, violence, and the unauthorized presence of firearms and alcohol, and will offer a disciplined environment conducive to learning.

Goal 8: Parental participation. By the year 2000 every school will promote partnerships that will increase parental involvement and participation in promoting the social, emotional, and academic growth of children (National Education Goals Panel [NEGP], 1991, p. 2).

Charting the course for the future educational reform, the governors' educational goals were solidified when Congress established the National Council on Education Standards and Testing in 1990. The purpose of the council was to answer the questions of what subject matter American students should know, how this knowledge should be assessed, and what performance standards should be set.

Subsequent to the establishment of the governors' educational goals, the National Council of Teachers of

Mathematics (NCTM) drafted *Curriculum and Evaluation Standards for School Mathematics* (NCTM, 1989). This report ushered in a new era of national organizations being involved in the practice of schooling (Kendall & Marzano, 2004). The mathematics standards helped form a new way of thinking about how national subject-area groups could contribute to the improvement of education.

The field of science soon followed. Scientists developed *National Science Education Standards* (National Research Council [NCR] and National Academy of Science [NAS], 1996). The science standards expanded the scope of standards by including standards for science teaching and professional development.

Other subject matter associations became involved. The National Center for History in the Schools (NCHS) published *National Standards for History* (NCHS, 1995), which included standards for history for Grades K–4 as well as standards for U.S. history and standards for world history for Grades 5–12. The Standards Project for the English Language Arts produced *Standards for the English Language* (National Council of Teachers of English [NCTE] and International Reading Association [IRA], 1995), and the Consortium of National Arts Education Associations (CNAEA) produced the document *Dance, Music, Theatre, Visual Arts: What Every Young American Should Know and Be Able to Do in the Arts* (CNAEA, 1994).

The fields of civics education, economics, foreign language, geography, health, physical education, social studies, technology, and the world of work followed with standards delineating what students should know and be able to do in these specific fields. Other nations and international organizations have also contributed to the standards movement. The Australian Education Council has produced standards; and the Third International Mathematics and Science Study (TIMSS), in addition to assessing students' knowledge of math and science, contributed a comparative study of math and science curricula to the standards movement (Martin & Kelly, 1998).

Professional associations and subject matter organizations were not alone in the development of standards. Federal, state, and local legislative bodies also have developed—and mandated—standards of learning and teaching in an effort to reform schools to raise the level of achievement for all children. By 1996, forty-nine states and the District of Columbia had developed a set of common standards in the core subject areas of math, English, the arts, social studies, and science (American Federation of Teachers [AFT], 1996). Although the mandates passed by different legislative bodies differ in scope, intent, clarity, or program focus, all are inspired by the vision of providing exemplary educational experiences that will enable all children to succeed and be productive members of a democratic society.

President George W. Bush renewed the call for standards and accountability in education. The No Child Left Behind Act (NCLB) of 2002 (U.S. Department of Education [US ED], 2004) is based on the concern that too many of the neediest children are left behind, despite the nearly $200 billion in federal spending since the passage of the Elementary and Secondary Education Act (ESEA) of 1965. The NCLB increases accountability for schools by calling for annual testing of all children in Grades 3–8, and annual statewide progress objectives ensuring that all groups of students reach proficiency within 12 years of schooling. Assessment results and state progress objectives must be broken out by poverty level, race, ethnicity, disability, and limited English proficiency to ensure that no group is left behind.

STANDARDS TODAY

National standards will continue to have salience in American education. There are at least three principal reasons for the development and use of standards (Kendall & Marzano, 2004): to establish clarity of curriculum content, to raise expectations for the achievement of all children, and to ensure accountability for public education.

Clarity

Standards bring clarity of content to the curriculum. The content that is being taught in today's schools does count: "The content of instruction plays a primary role in determining gains in student achievement" (Porter, 2002, p. 3). Students are more likely to learn if teachers teach content. This sounds like a truism, but the fact is that teachers have been the ultimate arbiters of what is taught and how. They make decisions about how much time to spend on a specific subject, which topics to include, and in what order (Porter, 2002).

The findings from the Third International Mathematics and Science Study (Martin & Kelly, 1998), showing that students in the United States achieve less in science and mathematics than do their counterparts in other nations, reinforced the call for standards and led to examining current curricula. High-scoring students were found to be from nations with national curricula. With standards-based curricula, students were able to master the core ideas in math and science.

The math and science curricula in this country could be characterized as including a bit of everything, but never going into depth in any one topic or concept. Thus critics maintain that the current math and science curricula are unfocused. Without the guidance provided

Standards have the potential to bring clarity
to the curriculum.

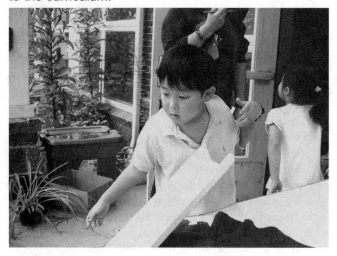

by standards, curriculum comes from a variety of texts or the teachers themselves. The proponents of standards claim that standards would focus the curriculum, presenting all students with a manageable set of concepts to be mastered within a given time.

Extending the argument, supporters of standards note that if standards are tied to accountability, teachers have more reason to teach a standardized curriculum. The result would be more standard achievement for students across the nation. As a result, students would be uniformly prepared to succeed in higher education and fully prepared to take their place as productive members of society.

Expectations

A second reason for standards is to raise expectations for student learning. In her book *National Standards in American Education: A Citizens Guide* (1995b), Diane Ravitch states that Americans expect strict standards

> to govern construction of buildings, bridges, highways and tunnels; shoddy work would put lives at risk. They expect stringent standards to protect their drinking water, the food they eat, and the air they breathe. . . . Standards are created because they improve the activity of life. (pp. 8–9)

Just as high expectations through standards are a part of daily life, Ravitch claimed, so should high expectations and standards be applied to education. Uniform standards for education would lead to the high expectations for the academic achievement of all students that Americans strongly support, believing that high expectations produce better academic perfor-

mance. Thus if students are expected to achieve, they will put greater effort into their schoolwork, which in turn will lead to higher achievement.

No Child Left Behind (US ED, 2004) reinforces the validity of holding high expectations for all children, regardless of socioeconomic background, race, or ethnicity. NCLB calls for implementing statewide accountability systems covering all public schools and students.

Although holding high expectations for each student, school, and school system is valid, problems still arise. Expectations can be unrealistic or unobtainable even with great effort. Current levels of student achievement and past student performance need to be taken into consideration when decisions about what is expected are being made (Linn, 2003).

Accountability

Today the movement to develop and implement standards of learning is closely tied to accountability. The success of standards, like any school reform, is ultimately tied to student performance. The NCLB Act (2002), Goals 2000 Act (1994), and other reform legislation emphasize the need for some well-defined means for reporting, and supporting, student progress. The term *accountability* implies a systematic method to assure those inside and outside the educational system that schools are moving toward those goals.

It is fair and necessary to account for students' achievement. First, because education is mandatory, society must be able to account for the effectiveness of its laws and regulations and for the monies spent on education. Then too, because education is given the

All children deserve access to the highest quality of education.

responsibility for preparing children to become productive members of a democracy, society must know how the children are being prepared. Accounting for students' learning allows changes to be made, faults to be corrected, and reforms designed to improve the quality of education to be implemented.

Thus accountability does have the potential to contribute to the improvement of education (Linn, 2003), if the accounting systems are designed with the following characteristics:

- They are based on valid research and theory about children, their growth development, and learning.
- They broadly define evidence of success, rather than defining success as a narrow set of academic skills.
- They have realistic expectations for young children.
- They lie within the context of what children already know and can learn.

IN SUMMARY

- Standards apply to nearly everything in our daily lives and are now being used in the field of education.
- Dissatisfied with the state of public schooling, various groups call for school reform. The current push for standards can be traced to 1957 when the Russians put Sputnik into space.
- The goals drawn up by the nation's governors at their Education Summit in 1989 initiated the standards movement.
- The National Council of Teachers of Mathematics and the science associations demonstrated the role of professional associations and organizations in school improvement by producing standards for their fields.
- Standards are here to stay. They serve to bring clarity to the curriculum, raise expectations for student learning, and provide a basis for accountability.

CHAPTER 2

Early Education and Standards

Standards for schools, for teacher preparation, and for the curriculum dominate the field of elementary and secondary education. As described in Chapter 1, since the mid-1950s public elementary and secondary education—what is taught and what children are to learn—has been influenced by school reform, accountability, and standards of learning. Until the beginning of the twenty-first century, the field of early childhood education remained aloof and relatively untouched by the mandates for school reform and the standards movement. The need, or desire, to identify in measurable ways what students should learn and be able to do was somewhat foreign to the field of early education.

The omission of the early learning years from the standards movement is the result of a number of factors. In the past those advocating and developing standards, whether for program quality, teacher preparation, or the curriculum, were focused solely on the education of children over the age of 5, not the very youngest of children.

The goals of the National Education Goals Panel (1991) did recognize the importance of early education in the first goal: "By the year 2000, all children will start school ready to learn." The focus of this goal, however, recommended only that young children have access to high-quality preschool programs, that parents be prepared to be their children's first teachers, and that children be physically healthy. The role of curriculum content was not a consideration.

The characteristics of the field itself—its diversity of programs and sponsorships—have kept the field distant from standards. The prevailing philosophy guiding the teaching and learning of young children has also negated the field's involvement in the national standards movement. In addition, early childhood teachers are generally autonomous and distant from standards, whether standards for program or for curriculum, and therefore may find it difficult to perceive curriculum standards as useful.

The goals of this chapter are to

- Discuss the reasons early childhood has been ignored in the standards movement
- Delineate current involvement of the field of early childhood in setting, implementing, and monitoring standards for programs, teacher preparation, and curriculum content
- Suggest guidelines for programs and teachers to maximize the usefulness of curriculum standards

CHARACTERISTICS OF THE FIELD OF EARLY CHILDHOOD EDUCATION

As noted, the field of early education has been separate from the standards movement. Young children, under the age of 5, are not included in national content area standards, nor in local or statewide curricula. With the exception of the mathematics standards, the national content area standards—like the state or local standards following the national standards—typically begin with kindergarten and define the period of early education as from kindergarten through Grade 4.

The omission of the education of children under the age of 5 is not surprising because the standards were developed in response to the elementary and secondary educational reform legislation. Addressing one of the major goals for education reform, the landmark legislation Goals 2000: Educate America Act (1994), mandated that all students will leave Grades 4, 8, and 12 having demonstrated competency over challenging subject matter in the core academic subjects of the school curriculum.

The panels of experts producing the national content standards were comprised of experts in the field, scientists, geographers, historians, artists, mathematicians, and others who could identify and delineate the structure and content of a given subject matter area.

Leaders in the field of elementary and secondary education were also included in the writing of subject matter standards. In general, then, those producing the standards were unfamiliar with the field of early education. Without knowledge of the field of early education, those developing standards did not consider what young children can and should learn during the years before entrance into kindergarten or the elementary schools, nor were they expected to do so.

Other factors, however, have negated the involvement of early educators in the standards movement. These include the wide age range of children served in a diversity of early childhood programs, the variety of sponsoring agencies, the field's separation from elementary education, and the philosophy of the field.

Wide Age Range and Diversity of Programs

Early childhood education is defined by the National Association for the Education of Young Children (NAEYC) as serving children from birth through age 8. Children with special needs from infancy through Grade 3 are also a part of early education. This may not be a wide age range in terms of years, but the differences between the education of an infant, a toddler, a preschooler, a 5-year-old, or an 8-year-old are vast.

Infants have very different educational needs than preschoolers, whose needs differ in turn from those of children who are 5 or 6 years old. These differences dictate different types of programs, methodologies, strategies, and regulations. No "one-size-fits-all" set of learning, program, or staffing standards would be effective in a field as diverse as early education.

Unlike public, or even private, elementary and secondary education, early childhood education is not a singular field. Rather it is made up of diverse programs. There are infant and toddler centers, nursery schools, preschools, child care centers, early learning programs for children with special needs, family child care, and prekindergarten and kindergarten programs, some which are in the public schools.

Sponsorship

While it is generally agreed that the education of children 5 years of age and older is the responsibility of the states, the education of younger children takes place under a variety of very different auspices—or not at all. Churches, community agencies, businesses, colleges and universities, corporations, and other agencies may sponsor programs and thereby have the prerogative of regulating and setting standards for their programs. Some early education programs may be funded and sponsored by local or state governments, as well as the federal government. Whatever regulations or program standards are implanted are specific and unique to the sponsoring agency.

The fact that great numbers of child care and early learning programs are privately owned and operated businesses must also be recognized. As private businesses, these programs are even more autonomous than those regulated by churches, agencies, or corporations. Privately owned and operated early childhood programs may have to meet state health requirements, but these are generally minimal regulations for providing basic health and safety equipment such as smoke detectors, fire extinguishers, and covers for electrical outlets.

As a field and in practice, early childhood programs stand alone. Of the 56,400 public elementary schools nationwide, only an estimated 28 percent were found to offer prekindergarten classes and 15 percent offered classes for prekindergarten children with special needs (NCES, 2003). Standards and regulations established by the public school system pertain only to those programs sponsored by school systems, and thus do not affect the majority of early childhood programs.

Autonomy

Early childhood programs, autonomous from public school regulations, gain even more autonomy from public education by being physically separated from elementary schools. Even prekindergarten, Head Start, and kindergarten programs located within a public school are often physically separated from the other grades in school buildings, perhaps housed in a separate wing of a building or in the basement (Lortie, 1975).

Even if early learning classrooms are integrated within a school building, early childhood teachers have autonomy from many public school and curriculum regulations and standards. Prekindergarten and kindergarten teachers have specialized training in early childhood education. Their methodologies differ from those of the elementary school teacher. The facts that teaching young children involves a great deal of physical care and that young children learn in very different ways than older children widen the distance between elementary and preschool teachers.

Early childhood teachers and programs have little or no collegiality with public school teachers or administrators. The only daily collegial and professional contact most early childhood teachers have is within their own small building and program. Thus early educators and elementary school teachers have little opportunity to share information. The give-and-take discussions about the role of standards or other school reforms taking place in the elementary school that might inform early childhood teachers of current trends does not take place. This does not mean that the early childhood community is not aware of standards; it does mean,

Early childhood teachers have a degree of autonomy.

however, that the opportunity to assimilate the idea of standards of learning into their existing ideas through free and open communication with others is missing (Spillane, Reiser, & Reimer, 2002). This is unfortunate since collaboration with other teachers about teaching and the curriculum is believed necessary to develop the shared responsibility required to implement school reforms such as content standards (Oakes, Quartz, Ryan, & Lipton, 2000).

Early Childhood Philosophy

Perhaps more important than physical separation from the public school, the field of early education is philosophically distant from the ideas motivating the standards movement. The field of early education is firmly based on a foundation of philosophies and theories of child development and constructivism. These are strong beliefs that children construct their own knowledge, albeit with experts who guide the development of this knowledge, that learning is a do-it-yourself process, and that teaching must be matched to the development of the child. These belief systems are philosophical barriers to accepting the idea of standards. The very idea of standards is incongruent with what the field knows and believes about how young children learn.

Early childhood educators, strongly influenced by maturation and constructivist theories, believe that what they want children to learn must match children's development (Bredekamp & Copple, 1997; Hunt, 1961; Vygotsky, 1986). Knowledge of child growth and development is necessary to match the curriculum or its goals and expectations for children's learning to the developmental capabilities of children (Seefeldt, 2005). When determining what children are to learn, teachers are encouraged to "focus on each of the children and the experiences, knowledge, skills, and interests each brings to the topic" (Katz, 2003, p. 11).

The idea that children's prior experience, their interests, and the resources of the community guide teachers' selection of content is not new. Lucy Sprague Mitchell (1934), a devotee of John Dewey's philosophy, advocated matching curriculum content not just to children's development, but to their here-and-now social and physical worlds. "The practical tasks for each school are to study the relations in the environment into which their children are born and to watch the children's behavior in their environment to note when they first discover relations and what they are" (p. 12). Then, based on knowledge of children and knowledge of the community in which they live, each teacher "makes her own curriculum for small children" (p. 12).

The book *Developmentally Appropriate Practice in Early Childhood Programs* (Bredekamp & Copple, 1997) illustrates the firmness of this foundation. First published in 1987 as *Developmentally Appropriate Practice in Early Childhood Programs Serving Children from Birth Through Age 8* (Bredekamp, 1987), this resource is based on the belief that a "major determinant of program quality is the extent to which knowledge of child development is applied in program practices—the degree to which the program is *developmentally appropriate*" (p. 2). The book describes developmentally appropriate practice across the full age span of early education and gives clear definitions of appropriate practices. The philosophy of the maturationists is clearly stated by Bredekamp:

> Development is a truly fascinating and wonderful phenomenon. It is not something to be accelerated or skipped. One period of early childhood or aspect of development is not better or more important than another; each has its own tasks to accomplish. (1987, p. iv)

The philosophy that children construct their own knowledge through physical, mental, and social activity is clarified in the 1997 edition. Bredekamp and Copple (1997) more fully articulate children's cognitive growth and development, and relate this development to language and mathematical learning.

Developmentally appropriate practice became the agreed-on theory guiding early education. State departments of education, the federal government, and agencies sponsoring child care programs embraced the philosophy that programs for children should be based on knowledge of child growth and development. They should be developmentally appropriate.

With the philosophy that development guides the curriculum, standards for learning and teaching were viewed as inappropriate by many. Thus the very idea that young children and their learning could be standardized like a pound of bananas is foreign to the field.

To others, standards in early childhood education represent a shove-down of the accountability pressures on elementary and secondary education (Hatch, 2002). This pressure for accountability is seen as having the potential to destroy the integrity of early childhood professionals and the quality of educational experiences for young children.

STANDARDS IN THE FIELD OF EARLY CHILDHOOD EDUCATION TODAY

Although a late comer, the field of early education has entered the world of standards and standard setting. The early childhood professional associations—the Association for the Childhood Education International (ACEI) and the National Association for the Education of Young Children (NAEYC)—have taken the lead in unifying the diverse and scattered field of early childhood education by issuing position statements and publishing and monitoring voluntary program standards, standards for teacher preparation, and curriculum standards. Federal, state, and local governments have also become involved in setting standards for programs for children under the age of 5.

Program Standards

NAEYC has established a voluntary accreditation system for early childhood programs serving children from birth through age 8. The purpose of *Accreditation Criteria and Procedures of the National Association for the Education of Young Children* (1998) is to improve the quality of child care and education provided for young children in group programs in the United States. The accreditation system is designed to meet two major goals:

- Engage early childhood personnel in a process that will facilitate real and lasting improvements in the quality of the programs serving young children
- Evaluate the quality of the programs for the purpose of accrediting those programs.

Established in 1985 and accrediting the first 19 programs in 1986, NAEYC has now accredited over 8,000 programs serving more than 700,000 children (NAEYC, 2003). It must be remembered, however, that the NAEYC accreditation program is voluntary. The numbers of children in accredited programs, although impressive, is just a fraction of those in early education programs nationwide.

Program standards for federally funded child care or other early education programs are in place. The Head Start reauthorization bill (U.S. Department of Health and Human Resources, 2004) sets new and higher standards for every facet of the Head Start program. Requirements and performance outcomes for academic, health, nutrition, parental involvement, social, and other Head Start services are delineated.

Teacher Preparation Standards

Nationally, there are no requirements for those who teach America's youngest children. To teach in a public elementary school, including kindergarten, teachers must hold at least a baccalaureate degree; but potentially anyone can be hired to teach in a child care center or other early learning program. Some programs, such as those sponsored by colleges or universities, may require a bachelor's or a master's degree. Yet other privately run programs may not even require teachers to have a high school diploma.

Because the quality of children's early learning experiences depends on the qualifications of the teacher, national associations have attempted to increase the quality of teacher preparation. ACEI (1998) in cooperation with the National Council for the Accreditation of Teachers (NCATE), prepared a position paper *Preparation of Early Childhood Education Teachers* that outlines program requirements for teacher preparation.

NAEYC has standards for initial licensure, advanced, and associate degree programs. *Preparing Early Childhood Professionals* (Hyson, 2003) is used to establish high standards for early childhood teacher education programs.

The Head Start reauthorization bill also includes new requirements for teacher preparation (USHHS, 2004). This bill mandates that by 2009 all center-based Head Start teachers must hold an associate degree or equivalent, and by 2010 at least 50 percent of Head Start teachers in center-based programs must have a baccalaureate degree relating to early childhood.

Curriculum Content Standards

The controversy over what young children should learn and be taught in an early education program—be

Standards for teacher education are in place.

it state or federally funded, privately owned, or operated by a school system—has long been an issue in the field of early childhood education (Seefeldt & Galper, 1998).

In the Froebelian kindergarten, instituted as a part of public education for 3-, 4-, and 5-year-old children in the St. Louis public schools in 1853, the curriculum consisted of "gifts and occupations" (Hill, 1902). The occupations were paper folding, weaving and perforation, bead stringing, and other crafts, and the gifts were things like balls, blocks, and cubes. Because the kindergarten was so popular, it quickly spread across the nation.

As it spread, new ideas and ways of thinking about how young children learned began to influence the curriculum. There were those who criticized the rigid, prescribed curriculum of Froebel, calling for play and a role for children to be more creative, such as making beds for paper dolls out of the Froebelian blocks (Hill, 1902).

Through the early 1900s the issues surrounding the early childhood curriculum revolved around whether the curriculum should be child-centered or prescribed. The behaviorists, influenced by the principles of behaviorism advanced by John B. Watson, advocated a cur-

riculum focused on teaching children habits of hand washing, dressing, and eating. At the other end of the continuum were those endorsing psychoanalytic theories advanced by the Yale Psycho-Clinic. These theories led to a curriculum of self-expression through play, finger paints, stories, music, and dance.

Debate over the nature of the curriculum accelerated during the 1960s with the advent of Head Start. Bereiter and Englemann's (1966) DISTAR, a program of direct instruction teaching letter and number names, was highly popular. In sharp contrast, the maturationists, spurred by theories of Piaget (1969), thought the curriculum should match children's developmental level. Embedded in activities and firsthand experiential learning, children would gain knowledge of the world around them.

What children should learn or be taught has yet to be resolved. Endorsed by the Bush administration (2001–2005) and pressured by the need to account for what children are learning, many are adopting a narrow, utilitarian view of education that focuses on children learning letter names and sounds. Today as in the past, the maturationists and constructivists continue to support a curriculum revolving around children's firsthand experiences.

Associations have advanced guidelines on what should be taught to young children. These guidelines are opposed to a narrow, utilitarian view of education, and continue to be grounded in maturational and constructivists theories. In 1992 and 1997 NAEYC published two volumes describing what children should learn and how. These books, *Reaching Potentials: Appropriate Curriculum and Assessment for Young Children* (Bredekamp & Rosegrant, 1992, 1997), were comprised of chapters written by authorities in different content areas. They described how and what to teach children in mathematics, science, social studies, and other subject matter disciplines.

More recently, NAEYC, with the National Association of Early Childhood Specialists in State Departments of Education (NAECS/SDE), published *Early Childhood Curriculum Assessment and Program Evaluation: Building an Effective, Accountable System in Programs for Children Birth Through Age 8* (2003), which identifies the features of effective early learning systems. These guidelines indicate that effective learning standards give emphasis to all domains of early development and learning, reflect meaningful and important ideas, and accommodate individual differences. The idea that what children learn must match children's individual development is prevalent in the guidelines.

Most states and the District of Columbia have developed early learning standards as well. As of 2003, only 11 states did not have standards or were not in the process of developing them (Kagan, Scott-Little, & Frelow, 2003). State standards vary greatly. Some state standards are designed for children during the preschool years, ages 3 to 5. Others have standards for children through kindergarten, and still other states have developed standards for toddlers (Kagan & Scott-Little, 2004). The content of the state standards varies widely as well. Some address social and emotional learning and children's approaches to learning, such as curiosity or persistence, and others do not. Missing from the state standards were children with special needs. "There was limited guidance on how standards were to be adapted for children with disabilities. Similarly, it was unclear from most of the documents how the standards were to be applied to children whose primary language is not English" (Kagan, Scott-Little, & Frelow, 2003, p. 60).

Standards of learning identifying the content that young children can and should learn may finally answer the question of what young children should be taught during the early years. CTB/McGraw-Hill, with the guidance of the Carnegie Corporation, developed *Pre-K Standards: Guidelines for Teaching and Learning* (2002). The standards are in the public domain and available on the CTB/McGraw-Hill Web site under "Resources"

The curriculum must match the nature of young children.

(http://www.CTB.com). Anne Lewis (2003) points out that these standards acknowledge that children's development and learning are interrelated—for example, learning cannot be separated from intellectual development—and emphasize that learning is embedded in children's culture and families. The framework defines what children should know and be able to do at each developmental level, describes the experiences children need to obtain this knowledge, and supports family involvement. "The CTB standards document is so thoughtful that it could mitigate the arguments over what happens in Head Start and other early childhood programs and give both proponents and critics something substantive to discuss" (Lewis, 2003, p. 99).

GUIDELINES FOR IMPLEMENTING EARLY CHILDHOOD STANDARDS

Clearly, it is time for the field of early education to identify what young children should learn. Standards of learning in early childhood education could improve children's early educational experiences and yield long-term benefits for the development and learning of the whole child (Wheatley, 2003).

Early learning standards could benefit early childhood education in several ways:

- Bring clarity to what young children can and should be learning, thus uniting the diverse field of early education
- Foster improvement in the development of curriculum for young children
- Bring continuity to young children's curriculum from preschool through the primary grades
- Help bring professionalism to the field
- Foster accountability among teachers for what they are teaching and what young children are learning

Changing early childhood teachers' autonomous position by asking them to follow a set of standards, however, may be problematic. Change is always difficult, but accepting standards as helpful instead of hurtful may be particularly troublesome for these teachers. To successfully implement standards in the field of early education will require both time and support for teachers.

Time

Change is always slow. Making the change from being in charge of what is taught to considering implementing content outlined in set standards will be especially difficult for teachers of young children. Teachers will need time for each part of this process:

- *Reading and reflecting on the standards.* Teachers will find that national content standards are generally congruent with developmentally appropriate practices and advocate for integrated learning through firsthand, meaningful experiences, as well as authentic assessment.
- *Meeting with experts in content areas and early education.* Teachers will learn how specific content area standards are best implemented in programs for young children.
- *Observing programs that implement standards.* Teachers will realize that standards do not negate creativity and thinking, and can be based on children's development and ways of learning.
- *Developing the motivation to change.* By studying standards, teachers will recognize the power standards have to bring direction and clarity to the curriculum.

Support

Everyone needs support when trying something new. Teachers will need the support of their peers, their programs, and the children's families when implementing standards (Spillane, Reiser, & Reimer, 2002).

When teams of teachers in a center work together to implement one or two specific standards in a given content area, they will feel supported. Administrators, directors, and principals provide another type of support. The leaders of a preschool may serve as cheerleaders and models, as well as providing mentor teachers and outside resources. Because the standards call for firsthand learning, they require materials, space, and equipment, all of which administrators can provide.

Sharing the responsibility for implementing standards-based education will be necessary. Increasing the quality of children's early educational experiences is the responsibility of the total community, not just teachers. The society as a whole, and individual families within it, provide the conditions that allow children to learn (Lewis, 2003). Involving families in reviewing and recommending standards brings shared responsibility and shared ownership in children's education. Locating resources outside the program for meeting specific content area standards brings community involvement. Program directors and state and local early childhood leaders can work together to build teams whose purpose is to discuss the characteristics and implementation of early childhood standards. Working with the elementary schools to ensure that early education standards are congruent with those of the elementary school offers children the potential of a continuous, whole curriculum that begins during their early years and continues throughout their elementary school experiences.

IN SUMMARY

- Standards, developed in response to calls for school reform and legislation demanding that children leave Grades 4, 8, and 12 with competency in subject matter, omitted the field of early education.
- The field of early childhood education distanced itself from the standards movement. The wide age range of children, the variety of programs and sponsors, and the autonomy of early childhood professionals, as well as their maturational and constructivist philosophies, kept the field from participating in the standards movement.
- Currently the field of early education has been involved in setting standards for programs, teacher preparation, and curriculum and assessment.
- Successful implementation of standards will require time, support, and shared responsibility.

PART II

SELECTING STANDARDS AND BENCHMARKS

CHAPTER 3

Evaluating and Selecting Standards

Since standards are now a part of early childhood education, professionals in the field need to consider seriously how they will approach standards. How standards are selected and used will determine whether they will foster quality early educational experiences for all children or work to negate the development of early educational programs of the highest quality.

The goals of this chapter are to

- Present guidelines for judging the validity of standards
- Analyze the content of standards
- Discuss the cultural relevance of standards and needs of special children
- Examine the congruence between standards in the field of early education with those developed for elementary education

JUDGING THE VALIDITY OF STANDARDS

Not only are standards here to stay, but there are more than enough of them. One teacher, presented with yet another set of standards, exclaimed, "Get real! No one could accomplish all of this with any group of children in just one year."

It is true; there are over 2,000 pages of national content standards and 14 pounds of documents (Marzano, 2002). Clearly, given the excess of standards, it will be necessary for early childhood educators to sort through, analyze, and make decisions about which standards will be incorporated into their program.

The Maze of Standards

There is a lot of confusion caused by the duplication of standards. First of all, there are standards for each of the content areas, from language learning to technology and everything in between. In many of these domains, there are multiple documents addressing standards (Kendall & Marzano, 2004). For example, standards for mathematics are delineated in *Principles and Standards for School Mathematics* (NCTM, 2000) but are also found in *Standards for Excellence in Education* (Council for Basic Education [CBE], 1998), *Mathematics Framework for the 1996 National Assessment of Educational Progress* (NAEP, 1996), and several other documents.

Another type of duplication occurs when standards for early learning have been developed at the state level as well as at the district or school system level. Still more duplication occurs when standards exist for specific programs, such as Head Start, or other early intervention programs.

There is also confusion as to which standards are mandated and which are voluntary, having been developed as guides or resources for teachers. For example, standards for early learning developed at the state level tend to be described as "expected," or "suggested." Even those using the words *mandated* or *required* may not have been legally legislated. Other standards are clearly voluntary. Their intent is to improve the quality of prekindergarten education in their state and bring continuity to children's early educational experiences (Kagan et al., 2003).

Regardless of the work and advice of professional associations, school administrators, or state departments of education, teachers will have to ask for themselves, "Which standards will guide my program?"

Judging standards on the basis of their validity and content, selecting standards, and providing for cultural relevance, inclusion, and congruence with elementary school standards give early educators methods for negotiating their way through the maze of standards. (See Figure 3.1 for guidance in sorting through standards.)

Teachers must ask how standards match their programs.

Authors of the Standards

Standards are developed and written by human beings, and therefore reflect the knowledge base and philosophy of those who wrote them. Being acquainted with the characteristics, beliefs, and knowledge of those who wrote the standards is critical to evaluating and selecting standards for use in a given program.

Generally, standards stemming from professional associations and organizations were written by scientists, experts, or authorities in the subject matter. Thus geographers, not educators, were involved in writing standards for geography education, mathematicians wrote the mathematics standards, and scientists, the

Figure 3.1. Sorting Through Standards

- *Go to the McREL web site* (http://www.mcrel.com). McREL (Mid-continent Research for Education and Learning) has analyzed the national content standards and benchmarks into 201 standards organized into 13 major categories.

- *Ask who actually wrote the standards.* Standards written by authorities in the field, or experts, have greater validity than those developed by novices. Experts will base decisions about key ideas and the structure of the content on research and theory, not on personal bias.

- *Think about the motives of those who developed the standards.* When the motives are understood, teachers will have a clearer idea of the intent of the standards and how they are to be implemented.

---

science standards. The committees and advisory boards, with their panels of experts guiding the development of the standards, rarely included more than one or two token teachers or educators. Since the national content standards were developed within the context of elementary and secondary school reform legislation, for the most part no early childhood educators were involved in the development of national subject matter standards.

Lacking the participation of early childhood professionals, many standards are highly impractical and unreasonable for use with young children. For example, it is unlikely that primary-aged children have the mental maturity to "compare climatic conditions in different regions of the world, taking into consideration factors such as distance from the Equator, elevation, and distance from cold or warm ocean current" (Geography Education Standards Project [GESP], 1994, p. 119). The standards for civics education, which call for third graders to be able to explain the most important responsibilities of each branch of the government (Center for Civic Education [CCE], 1994, p. 19) or to "name the persons representing them at state and national levels in the legislative branches of government" (p. 21), is another example of standards that illustrate unrealistic ideas of young children's thought processes.

Instead of helping teachers identify key concepts in a given discipline area and use standards as a guide for planning and selecting curriculum content, some standards overwhelm teachers. For instance, the geography standards are so multidimensional, both in breadth and depth, it would take years for any group of children to master any given subset of the standards.

Goals of the Sponsoring Groups

When evaluating standards, it is important not only to understand the background and values of the authors of the standards but those of the sponsor or association promoting the standards as well. Understanding the social forces, politics, goals, and philosophies of the association, legislative body, or organization funding the development of standards is critical to judging and using standards.

For example, the goal of state departments of education in developing standards for early education may be to bring quality to the burgeoning, unsupervised field of early education (Kagan et al., 2003). Or the purpose may be to create consistency and continuity of young children's educational experiences as they move from child care to preschool and through kindergarten and the first three grades. Departments of education may conclude that consistency and continuity of curriculum would serve to enhance children's achievement once in the public school system.

State departments of education may have other goals for developing standards for preschool education. Their involvement in child care and preschool education might bring substance and credibility to the field of early education. Just the delineation of what young children can and should learn as toddlers and preschoolers is likely to enhance child care workers' and preschool teachers' knowledge of both subject matter and how children learn, which in turn would lead to programs of higher quality. Thus when children enter public school, they would be better prepared for academic success.

Associations or organizations promoting standards may be guided by any number of goals. Since science and mathematics achievement were singled out by the National Education Goals Panel (1991), the National Council of Teachers of Mathematics and the science associations responded quickly by developing goals and standards. Professional associations not under pressure, such as the Consortium for Arts Education, developed standards much later.

ANALYZING THE CONTENT OF THE STANDARDS

The purpose of standards is to delineate the content children are to learn. The standards should describe the information and skills children are to attain at a given grade level (Kendall & Marzano, 2004). Nevertheless, some standards are written in ways that convey specific goals for children's learning and how children are to achieve these goals, as well as principles of curriculum development.

In analyzing standards early educators can ask these questions:

- Which standards are procedural, declarative, or contextual?
- Are these content standards, or are they curriculum standards?
- Are the information and skills that children are to gain clearly stated?

How Standards Are Written

Standards may be written as declarative, procedural, or contextual. *Declarative* standards are composed of information important to a given content area. Such standards state the facts students are to understand, such as the concepts of amoeba, geographic region, or location.

Standards that describe what students are to do or perform can be classified as *procedural*. The presumption of these standards is that if the students can per-

form the specified task, they have acquired the prerequisite information and skills specified for this topic. Standards that indicate students are to classify, identify, analyze, read, perform a task, set up an experiment, or execute a specific task or activity are examples of procedural standards (Kendall & Marzano, 2004).

Still other standards are *contextual. Contextual knowledge* is defined as information acquired during the execution of some process. Standards that are contextual typically "begin with verbs or verb phrases but tend to look more like activities in that a particular skill is described in terms of information or knowledge about or upon which the skill is applied" (Kendall & Marzano, 2004).

Adapting Content Standards

In the past, teachers of young children had little information about what children could and should learn by a given age. Teachers generally have adequate information about children's growth and development and what children know and can do as a result of maturation, but exactly what they should teach and children learn is often unclear. When asked what content they are teaching, early childhood educators often respond by saying, "I teach children, not subjects."

Standards in given subject areas that define the content, information, and skills children can learn at a given age will strengthen teachers' understanding of the teaching-learning process. It must be remembered, however, that the national content standards begin delineating what children should know and be able to do at the kindergarten level. Content area standards are generally divided into the age groups of K–Grade 4, Grades 5–8, and Grades 9–12. Instead of delineating what children should know in a subject area at the end of kindergarten and Grades 1, 2, and 3, the standards state what children should know at the end of Grade 4. Because standards delineate what fourth graders should know and be able to do, early childhood educators will have to fill in the blanks. Using the fourth-grade standard as the goal, early childhood educators will have to create the road map of content to get to the goal.

Yes, teachers of young children will always place children before subject matter, but now with knowledge of what children can learn of a given discipline area by the end of fourth grade, they can confidently select content for young children's learning. Knowledge of what children should achieve by the end of fourth grade can guide teachers' curriculum development and enable them to interact with children in more intentional ways (see Figure 3.2).

Teachers are still faced with the question, "What of this content matches the interests, needs, abilities, and

Figure 3.2. Negotiating Standards

Knowledge of young children, their growth development, and their here-and-now environment, coupled with knowledge of standards from each content area, lead teachers to

- *Find out which set of standards are operational in their program.* Teachers can ask administrators or curriculum directors to be specific about which set of standards to follow.

- *Ask "who said so?"* Finding out who mandated these standards might be illuminating. In some cases, teachers are unable to trace the source to any one person or office and reach the realization that rumors led to the idea that a specific set of standards was mandated.

- *Enter into a dialogue with the originators of the standards.* Teachers can, without confrontation, question unrealistic expectations or inappropriate demands, and work to create standards that are usable in their specific situation.

---

strengths of the children I teach?" Attacking this question from five different angles will help teachers select specific standards.

1. *From this body of knowledge and subject matter, what holds meaning for the group of children I am working with? Which is age appropriate for these children?* Knowledge of subject matter develops gradually. Children have a long time to grow and learn. In order to gain the information found in the standards, children will need to experience similar ideas and content through their everyday, meaningful experiences. For example, if teachers want children to learn concepts of measurement, children will first have to experience measurement. Preschoolers will have to have many opportunities to pour sand or water from one container to another. First graders might get involved in weighing different containers filled with sand or water and determine which container is heavier. Second graders could determine which container holds the most, and what happens when sand or water is poured into a different-shape container.

2. *What element or elements of this specific standard or content does a novice learner need to know?* In other words, teachers must differentiate between what a competent, proficient, or expert learner would know about a subject and what a young child needs to know, un-

derstand, or discover. In other words, teachers might ask, "What does a child of 3, 5, or 7 years of age need to know now? What can be learned more efficiently when the child is older and can actually use the knowledge gained?"

3. *What do children already know about the concept or content I want them to learn?* What children are being asked to learn must be related to what they already know. The teachers' job is to find out what children do know about a given skill or idea, then match their teaching to children's knowledge in ways that help children clarify, extend, and expand their ideas, and develop more accurate, conventional ideas.

Finding out what children know of a given topic is not that easy. Young children will not be able to tell all they know of a subject. Teachers have to observe children using the concepts or content they want to teach children. For example, young children are unable to articulate what cooperation means. Nevertheless, they do cooperate.

Although 6- and 7-year-olds do not understand the abstract concepts of mapping such as scale and orientation, and are not able to interpret a map using the key, they do draw maps and use them to find hidden treasure or places on the play yard and in their neighborhood. Using children's present knowledge of maps, teachers can introduce them to scale, orientation, and other mapping skills.

4. *What aspects of this standard or content can be introduced to children through their firsthand experience in the classroom or through field experiences?* The Web site *Journey North* (Annenberg/CPB, 2004) presents children with a global study of wildlife migration; enables children to follow a variety of plants, insects, and animals through their migration; makes use of children's firsthand experiences, as well as the vicarious. For instance, children keep in touch with children from Mexico to Canada, viewing the migration of Monarch butterflies. When the butterflies migrate to their area, children take photos, make drawings, conduct scientific experiments, and communicate their findings to others on the Web site. In the process, children are melding their firsthand experiences with the firsthand experiences of others, and bringing meaning to the vicarious.

5. *How can a concept or content be integrated with what children have already experienced or learned in the preschool, kindergarten, or previous grades?* Children in one port city visit the harbor each year. Preschoolers watch the boats and take a short ride around the harbor. They draw, dance, write, read books, and talk about their experiences. In successive years teachers ask children what they remember about their previous trips to the harbor and what they want

Knowledge of children guides selection of appropriate standards.

to investigate further this year. By the third grade, children investigate such things as where the ships come from, the products ships bring and take from the harbor and where these are going, the weight of different products, the concept of floating, and jobs related to the harbor.

CONSIDERING CULTURAL APPROPRIATENESS AND INCLUSION

The word *standard*, which means the usual approved model, connotes commonality. A concern about standards of learning is this idea of commonality. Inherent in the standards is the idea that all children are the same and all children will attain the information and skills at the same time. Depending on how standards are used and implemented, children's individuality and culture could readily be ignored. When selecting standards—or implementing mandated standards—teachers will want to consider how the standards do, or can be modified to, accommodate cultural differences and the needs of individual children.

Because the purpose of standards is to outline content, information, and skills children are to learn, they should bring a measure of cultural neutrality with them. Knowledge of numerals, the characteristics of objects, or the use of maps and globes seem relatively culture free. But even though the outline of content may be culture free, it may not be culturally fair. What teachers ask children to learn—the content—as well as the methods they choose for presenting the content are ultimately embedded in the predominant culture of the nation. Some people even claim that content standards are based on Eurocentric and male-centric values and

thus ignore the experiences, voices, contributions, and perspectives of nondominant individuals and groups in all subject areas (Gorski, 2003).

Still, how the standards are operationalized and translated into actual practice will depend on teachers. Regardless of whether or not standards are mandated, they do not mandate *how* children are to gain specific knowledge. The methods and strategies used to help children attain this knowledge will be up to teachers who are skilled in adjusting strategies and methodologies to meet the needs of individual students and specific groups of students.

Skilled teachers ensure that a curriculum guided by standards of learning does not have negative consequences for children from nondominant groups. They make adaptations in their program to accommodate children from different cultures and children with special needs.

Including Children from Different Cultures

Skilled teachers do everything they can to understand the culture and values of the children they teach. They talk with families about what children do at home, how they celebrate holidays, and most important, about what their goals are for their children and how they think the school can help them achieve these goals.

Teachers take the time to drive around the neighborhood and note the things children experience. They observe whether there are supermarkets or grocery stores in the neighborhood, *la marketas* or *la tiendas*; what plants are common to the area; what types of buildings are there and what they are made of. Their point is to find out what children are familiar with, the vocabulary they use, and incorporate it into the curriculum of the school.

Reading about the home culture of children, talking with people from the culture, or consulting experts in the culture help teachers better understand children, their learning styles, values, and thinking processes.

Celebrate diversity. Regardless of whether the children share the same culture or not, a goal of early education is to teach the value of diversity. It follows that the materials of the school will be representative of a diversity of cultures. Books, posters, other written material, and computer software will depict children of many differing ethnic and racial groups. Materials and props for dramatic play will be chosen to reflect children's home cultures. One teacher found that adding woks and chopsticks to the dramatic play area fostered a great deal of language and interaction between two Chinese children and the other children in the group.

A goal of early education is to teach the value of diversity.

Use children's here-and-now world. Long ago Lucy Sprague Mitchell (1934) wrote that each school must create its own curriculum. Her idea was that children's here-and-now world is meaningful to children. By studying this world, children could be appropriately introduced to complex concepts of their world. She was right. Research shows that when children's minds and hands are engaged in study of their world, children will learn (NRC, 2001b).

Study of children's here-and-now world guarantees a measure of cultural appropriateness. If addressing the science standard *children will develop an understanding of the diversity of life,* the teacher could take the class on a walk around the block and identify different plants, naming them and observing where and how they grow. These plants could be compared with those from the children's home environment. To supplement children's actual firsthand experiences, teachers can introduce books about plants from other regions or invite families to bring photographs or tell stories of plants they know.

Including Children with Special Needs

Perhaps because standards state content children are to learn, not how they are to learn this, children with special needs are generally not considered in most of the national subject matter standards. Standards for early learning developed at the state level also seem to be based on the belief that these standards are intended to be applicable to all children, including those with special needs. Exactly how the standards will apply to children with special needs is less clearly articulated (Kagan et al., 2003).

To meet special needs, teachers may need to think of time differently. With the assumption that all children develop and learn at the same rate, the standards specify when children are to attain specific content. In addressing the Individual Educational Plans (IEPs) of children with special needs, many of the standards can be included, but the time in which children are to attain these may not be congruent with that specified in the standards.

Depending on the needs of specific children, other accommodations will need to be made. The following suggestions can guide teachers in including children with special needs within their programs:

- Arrange the physical environment to accommodate the special needs of children
- Provide consistency of schedules and structure to help all children develop a sense of security
- Use cooperative learning groups to allow children to acquire social as well as academic skills
- Individualize instruction through theme-based, integrated curriculum
- Present instruction in a way that every child, no matter what the special need is, can assimilate information and develop important skills
- Partner children with each other to gain a specific standard

DEVELOPING CONGRUENCE WITH ELEMENTARY STANDARDS

The standards movement is fostered by the belief that a standardized curriculum, implemented from kindergarten through secondary school, will enhance children's achievement. Findings from the Third International Mathematics and Science Study (Martin & Kelly, 1998) suggests that when nations implement standard mathematics and science curricula, students' achievement increases.

Standards developed at the state level for early learning are also based on the premise that children will benefit from continuity of curriculum. When the curriculum of a child care or preschool setting provides foundational information for kindergarten and primary classes, it is assumed that children will benefit. Children would not be asked to repeat information or skills already attained, nor would they be presented with concepts that have no meaning to them.

In selecting standards for early learning that will apply to a specific program, teachers will have to obtain standards from the school district. These are usually published on the school district's Web site, or they can be obtained through transition committees set up by the schools.

Then, with committees or individuals assigned to specific content areas, teachers can check to see which of the early childhood standards would provide children information and skills prerequisite to the kindergarten or primary standards. One child care program taught children to recognize capital letters. On reviewing the school district's standards of learning for kindergarten, the group noted that upon entrance into kindergarten children were expected to be able to recognize lowercase letters. Since then the program has integrated letter learning into the entire curriculum, including lowercase letters. Thus this standard was easily and readily addressed.

IN SUMMARY

- Any given subject area has numerous standards, and there is duplication of standards within subject areas. States and local systems have also developed standards.
- Early childhood professionals are faced with the task of selecting from the standards. They will judge and analyze standards for appropriateness of use with the children they teach.
- Standards were written for kindergarten through Grade 4, with the knowledge to be gained delineated for children at the end of Grade 4. With these standards to guide them, teachers will have to delineate content for young children.
- Teachers will need to consider the cultural appropriateness of standards.
- Standards will need to be modified to meet the special needs of all children.
- Standards could be selected with the goal of promoting continuity of curriculum from preschool through the early grades.

CHAPTER 4

Working with Benchmarks

The authors of standards in the different content areas define standards differently. The definition for *standard* and the way standards are expressed vary not just between different statements of standards but within standards documents for a given content area (Kendall & Marzano, 2004). While groups differ in their definition of a standard, most would agree that there is a need to identify the skill, knowledge, or understanding that is expected at a given developmental level or point in time. For example, a standard may be something as broad as "solves a math problem." The associated benchmarks would then describe what this means at each grade or developmental level. *Benchmarks*, sometimes referred to as *performance standards* or *outcomes*, define the content children are to know in a given discipline or what they should be able to do at the end of a given period of study.

Early childhood educators are concerned that benchmarks could become items on a standardized test, which in turn would lead to a standardized curriculum with every child expected to learn the same thing at the same time and be tested in the same way. This is not the case, however. Standards and their benchmarks delineate content but do not prescribe how children are to learn this content. Nor can benchmarks be easily translated into standardized tests or a standardized curriculum. In fact, the benchmarks accompanying standards have the potential to make meaningful, personalized assessment the norm. Both standards and their benchmarks call for authentic methods of assessing. Instead of asking children to sit and take a standardized, pencil-and-paper test, benchmarks call for a range of meaningful assessment techniques.

The goals of this chapter are to

- Examine the nature of benchmarks and bring clarity to knowledge of benchmarks
- Offer educators guidelines for judging benchmarks and suggestions for using them
- Enable teachers to bring congruence between the benchmarks and children's developmental levels

- Provide information on how to select and implement appropriate methods of assessing benchmarks

EXAMINING BENCHMARKS

Benchmarks vary in specificity and content. Like standards, benchmarks can be declarative, procedural, or contextual (Kendall & Marzano, 2004). Declarative benchmarks generally include words such as *recognize, identify, recall, describe*, or *name*. The word *declare* means to say, speak out, or state. Procedural benchmarks use words such as *do* or *make*. The word *procedure* means process, method, or action. Contextual benchmarks call for students to apply, communicate, explain findings, make and investigate, determine proof, and judge within a given content (Porter, 2002). (See Figure 4.1 for examples of benchmarks.)

Benchmarks are not behavioral objectives (Kendall & Marzano, 2004). Behavioral objectives require much greater specificity than typical benchmarks offer. *Behavioral objectives*, as described by Mager (1962), require stating a target behavior, what the student will be able to do, criteria for acceptable performance, and the conditions under which the behavior will be demonstrated. Benchmarks are broader than objectives and could be the source of many behavioral objectives (Kendall & Marzano, 2004).

Vagueness

Because of the broadness of benchmarks, many seem vague and amorphous instead of precise and specific. The K–4 mathematics benchmark that students will "develop number sense" (NCTM, 1989, p. 37), leaves much to the teacher to determine what constitutes number sense and how children will demonstrate knowledge of number sense. The K–4 history benchmark "demonstrate understanding of the history of their local community" (NCHS, 1994) is typical of the vagueness of many benchmarks.

Figure 4.1. Examples of Standards and Benchmarks

Mathematics

Standard: The study of mathematics should emphasize reasoning (NCTM, 1989, p. 29).

Benchmark: Children will describe their answers and solution processes (K–Grade 4).

Visual Arts

Standard: The ability to choose a range of subject matter, symbols, and ideas (CNAEA, 1994, p. 34).

Benchmark: Children will select and use subject matter, symbols and ideas to communicate meaning (K–Grade 4).

Geography

Standard: The location of major physical and human features in the United States and on Earth (GESP, 1994, p. 108).

Benchmark: Children will use historical data, primary and secondary documents, illustrations and sources of information to describe changes in a cultural characteristic (e.g., the role of children in society, clothing styles, modes of transportation, food preferences, types of housing, attitudes toward the environment and resources) (K–4).

State departments of education, various associations, and others have filled in some of the blanks in vaguely stated standards. Regardless, the benchmarks that result from the efforts of state departments of education and other agencies to bring clarity to benchmarks are still problematic. Developed without sufficient time for research, and perhaps with limited funds, some of the resultant benchmarks seem to be arbitrary, unrealistic, and developmentally inappropriate (Kendall & Marzano, 2004). For example, the Head Start performance standard for 4-year-olds that "children will learn the names of 10 letters" leads to several questions: Why 10 letters? Do 4-year-olds need to learn letter names now? How can they use this knowledge? Is this something children can learn with ease when they are 5 years old? What research supports the idea that learning 10 letters is somehow better than learning 5 or 11?

A Point in Time

Benchmarks are just that—a mark of what children should achieve at one point in time. The prerequisite knowledge—how to get there—is open to interpretation. This means teachers are in control of what children will learn and how that learning will be assessed. Teachers are the ones who will have to determine what children will need to know and be able to perform prior to achieving a benchmark. Teachers, as Lucy Sprague Mitchell (1934) suggested, will have to plan an individualized curriculum for each child and each group they teach. They will be the curriculum designers and the curriculum evaluators because they are the ones who will determine the steps that will lead to achieving the benchmark.

For example, teachers will have to take the mathematics standard and its benchmark "students can describe, model, draw, and classify shapes" (NCTM, 1989, p. 48), and ask themselves, "What do children need to learn before they can describe, model, draw, and classify shapes?" Breaking this benchmark into steps, teachers would realize that before children could achieve the benchmark, they would first have to be able to

- Recognize and name individual shapes such as squares, circles, triangles, and rectangles

How to get to the benchmarks is open to interpretation.

- Compare and contrast shapes
- Articulate differences in shapes
- Classify based on more than one characteristic (e.g., shape and color)
- Have the mental maturity required to draw shapes (e.g., drawing a triangle requires a mental age of 7)

Age Range

Benchmarks are troublesome in other ways as well. Typically, benchmarks are given for a specific range of grades, such as for kindergarten through Grade 4 (see the examples in Figure 4.2), but they generally state what students are to achieve at the upper end of the range, such as Grade 4. This means that benchmarks unique to the earlier grades—prekindergarten, kindergarten, and Grades 1, 2, and 3—are rarely identified.

MATCHING BENCHMARKS TO CHILDREN'S DEVELOPMENTAL LEVELS

When selecting benchmarks, teachers need to see how congruent a benchmark is with children's development. This chapter's appendix provides a list of developmental milestones—indications of what children of a given age can typically do, understand, and learn. In considering each benchmark, teachers will have to answer questions about three aspects of development:

- *What prior knowledge, skills, and abilities will children need to achieve the benchmark?* Teachers should look at a benchmark and a list of developmental milestones, and compare the skills required for the benchmark with those typically possessed by children of a given age.
- *Is this benchmark something children need to know now?* Is this something children need and can use right now, or is it something they will not need to use until later in life? For instance, when would children need to know and analyze the location of places (see Figure 4.2)?
- *Is this something children can learn with ease and efficiency now or will it take a great deal of time, teaching, practice, and reinforcement for children to learn?* Children can learn to memorize answers to specific questions or count to a given number, but how much time, energy, and effort on the part of children and adults will it take? Is it a wise use of time and energy to try to teach this to young children now? Or is this something children could learn with ease later after more experience and with greater maturity?

Benchmarks vary widely. Some set expectations that are too high or too low for children. Benchmarks that are

Figure 4.2. Judging Benchmarks

Based on knowledge of child growth and development, which of the following K–4 benchmarks are appropriate for children in preschool, kindergarten, first, second, or third grade?

Theatre

Writing scripts by planning and recording improvisations based on personal experience and heritage, imagination, literature, and history (CNAEA, 1994, p. 30).

Science

Matching pictures of instruments used to measure weather conditions with the condition the instrument measures (NCR/NAS, 1996, p. 136).

Mathematics

Interpreting the multiple uses of numbers encountered in the real world (NCTM, 1989, p. 38).

Dance

Understanding choreographic principles, processes, and structures (CNAEA, 1994, p. 24).

Geography

Analyzing the location of places and suggesting why particular locations are used for certain human activities (GESP, 1994, p. 131).

Too high lead to stress and failure.
Too low encourage mediocrity.
Too specific negate creativity and diversity.
Too broad are meaningless. (Burns, Bodrova, Leong, & Midgette, 2001)

In selecting standards and judging benchmarks, early childhood educators will have to assume the role of protectors of young children's rights to be children. State departments of education develop standards for prekindergarten programs. These stem from existing standards for children in kindergarten and the elementary grades. Local county agencies in charge of child care and preschool licensing also develop standards. Far too often, both sets of standards are based on what elementary children should know and be able to do and focus on a narrow set of academic skills. These skills, for young children, typically revolve around learning the names of letters and letter sounds.

Too often, the child care community, wanting to do the best for the young children they serve, change their cognitive-rich curricula to curricula designed to "prepare" children to achieve the prekindergarten or kindergarten standards. To do so, the kindergarten curriculum is watered down to become the curriculum for the preschool. In turn, the preschool curriculum is watered down to become the curriculum for the toddlers. As a result, children are denied the opportunity to live and learn in age appropriate ways. Instead of building foundations of concepts, literacy, and language learning, children are expected to learn academic skills that have no meaning to them.

Teachers will need to resist the "dribble-down" curriculum. They can do so by being able to articulate what young children can and should learn at a given age. Illustrating and demonstrating what children are learning, and how they are learning it, helps protect them from a meaningless, watered-down version of a curriculum meant for older children.

USING BENCHMARKS AS TOOLS FOR ASSESSMENT

The mathematics, geography, history, arts, and science standards are all based on the assumption that children are active learners. Each of the standards takes the position that young children are active individuals who construct, modify, and integrate ideas by interacting with their physical world, materials, and other children (NCR/NAS, 1996; NCTM, 1989). Thus the standards make clear that children learn through their active exploration of their world (CNAEA, 1994; GESP, 1994).

The authors of the standards agree that benchmarks must involve children in activity as well. Nowhere throughout the standards are standardized measures mentioned as a possible way to assess children's achievement of the benchmarks. Rather, children are expected

Protect children's right to be children.

to be actively involved and engaged in meaningful assessment experiences that require children to

Justify	Develop
Represent	Apply
Solve	Describe
Construct	Discuss
Use	Interpret
Investigate	Draw/Write/Dance

Benchmarks are most likely to be procedural, as in the content standard for music that calls for children to demonstrate a specific skill such as sing, alone and with others, a varied repertoire of music; sing independently, on pitch and in rhythm; sing expressively, with appropriate dynamics, phrasing, and interpretation; and sing in groups, blending vocal timbres (CNAEA, 1994).

Likewise, benchmarks from *A Framework for Early Literacy Instruction* (Bodrova, Leong, Paynter, & Semenov, 2000) are based on children's ability to complete tasks, not on standardized tests. These benchmarks ask children to identify the most salient sound in a spoken word and attempt to represent it in writing, know how to handle printed materials, and recognize a few letters. The mathematics standards, as well, call for students to use problem-solving approaches, formulate problems from everyday life, and verify and interpret results (NCTM, 1991).

The point is that benchmarks typically call for students to explain, define, or actually do something to demonstrate attainment of the benchmark. Virtually none of the subject matter disciplines developed by professional associations indicate that achievement of benchmarks is to be documented through standardized testing. Rather, idiographic and authentic methods of assessment—those that actually paint a picture of an individual child's understanding and attainment of a given benchmark—are the norm. For example, the science standards call for authentic assessment tasks. Students are to be engaged in assessment tasks that are similar in form to tasks in which they will engage in their lives outside the classroom, or are similar to the activities of scientists (NCR/NAS, 1996).

In agreement with early childhood educators, authorities in the subject matter disciplines recognize that young children are not good test takers. Young children have neither the physical nor mental maturity to fill in bubbles or mark responses on some form of coding sheet. Nor are they able to sit still or understand the nature of testing. Andrea, entering kindergarten, returned home telling her mother she was the smartest kid in the class. When asked why she thought this, Andrea said, "The teacher passed out tests, and I got mine first and finished it even before the other kids got theirs." Some children, not understanding directions, mark all the circles in a given column. One child when asked why he had filled in the squares as he did said, "We learned about making patterns, and I made a pretty pattern."

In general the authors of standards would agree that assessment should

- Be planned
- Have explicitly stated purposes
- Be authentic, an integral part of the curriculum
- Match the curriculum
- Be free from stereotypic images and language
- Include multiple methods

Teachers, to assess children's attainment of benchmarks, are asked to do four things:

- Observe children
- Interview children
- Ask children to perform a task
- Analyze samples of children's work

Observations

The seemingly simple act of observing can reveal a great deal about children. Unlike a standardized test that assesses children's knowledge of a predetermined, narrowed number of facts or skills, observations can yield a multitude of information. How children learn and what they have learned, can do, understand, and know can be documented through informal and formal observations (Copley, 2000).

Informally and spontaneously, teachers observe children's activities and interactions (Seo, 2003). They listen to children talk, noting their constructive errors to better understand children's thinking, and informally make judgments about children's strengths and weaknesses: "She did that well" or "He counted all the blocks with one-to-one correspondence." These informal and spontaneous reflections on the events and occurrences of the day can be used to assess achievement of benchmarks (Dodge, Heroman, Charles, & Maiorca, 2004). See Figure 4.3 for an example of one teacher's observations with benchmarks noted.

Still, more formal and structured observations will be necessary to document individual children's attainment of benchmarks. Teachers might elect to observe children's attainment of a specific benchmark by using event sampling. The teacher—selecting a benchmark, perhaps "construct number meanings through real-world experiences and the use of physical materials" (NCTM, 1989, p. 38)—might focus observations only on the events of counting or use of place value, both of which are essential for constructing number meanings through real-world experiences.

Figure 4.3. Using Informal Observation to Assess Achievement

Informal, spontaneous observation	Benchmark
Shwana spent a lot of time at the manipulatives table. She sorted the shape blocks into baskets.	Recognize shapes.
Children playing shoe store decided who would be the clerk and then found paper, scissors, and markers to make paper money to pay for shoes.	Exchange money for goods or services.
Madison "read" a book of nursery rhymes to the baby doll. When she finished, she said, "That should do it," as she slammed the doll in the bed.	Use reading for a variety of purposes.

Keeping the benchmark in mind, the teacher would note instances of children counting or using knowledge of place value as they build with blocks, play store, work with art materials, or read books. The child's name, the conditions under which counting took place, and the child's actual counting or use of place value would be recorded on a note card for each child. After observing children's use of number over several days, the teacher would organize the note cards into a computer file and reach conclusions about children's understanding of counting.

First-grade teachers may want to know how children are attaining the benchmark of "checking their solution to a difficult word against their knowledge of print-sound correspondences and the meaning of the text" (New Standards, 1999, p. 102). They could record events in which children try to read a word such as *flake* by trying other words, *flip* and *fake*, then read to the end of the sentence to see what makes contextual sense.

Other benchmarks might better be observed through time sampling. For example, benchmarks revolving around children speaking and listening to others, using language in a variety of ways, or using specific number concepts might lend themselves to time sampling. Using time-sampling techniques, a teacher might decide to observe children's language usage every 5 minutes during free play. Then every 5 minutes the teacher would stop, observe what children are doing and saying, and record her observations.

Assessment is authentic when it is a part of the curriculum.

Anecdotal observations are useful. Keeping in mind specific benchmarks, teachers would record instances when children spontaneously demonstrate attainment of a benchmark. Thus a teacher, observing a child dividing cookies among the dolls in the housekeeping area, would record the event and later incorporate it into the child's computer file as an illustration of the child's developing number sense.

Beginning readers' understanding, skills, and knowledge of phonemic awareness, letter-sound correspondence, and other early reading skills are observed through running records. As children read, teachers observe and record each word the child reads correctly as well as children's use of any number of reading skills.

Narrative observations of what children are doing and saying might be used when the goal is to describe children. Narrative observations were used as the basis of *Social Worlds of Children Learning to Write in an Urban Primary School* (Dyson, 1993). In another study narratives of play situations revealed children's spontaneous use of knowledge and literacy (Roskos & Christie, 2002). Through observations of children at play children's procedural and declarative knowledge and skills were made visible in their role taking and problem solving.

Educational researchers, state departments of education, or local school districts might create rating scales based on standards and their benchmarks. Teachers would observe individual children, or the group, and rate the extent to which children are demonstrating specified behaviors. Rating scales reduce some of the subjectivity found in other more informal observational methods. The scales are stable over time and can predict future child outcomes and behaviors.

With current technologies, more sophisticated observations are possible. Through the use of audio- and videotapes, computers, and digital cameras, teachers can keep a permanent record of children's attainment of specific benchmarks. The permanence of the observations makes possible multiple analyses and approaches to observations (Seefeldt & Galper, 1998).

Despite the usefulness of observations, there are problems with the methodology. Observations are always biased. Everything one observes, even what one chooses to observe, passes through the filter of the observer's mind. The issues of reliability and validity—can the same results be obtained over time and are these results accurate—pertain to using observation as an assessment tool.

Interviews

Nearly every adult has been interviewed at one time or another—for entrance into college, for a job, or by a physician. It seems surprising, given the widespread use of interviews with adults, that interviews are not more widely used to assess young children's learning. Especially since it was the interview that changed the way we understand children's thinking. In his pioneering research on children's thinking, Piaget (1969) demonstrated, not only how to interview children, but the wealth of information interviewing young children can yield.

Interviews have a number of features that make them an ideal tool for assessing children's attainment of benchmarks. The interview—interaction between a teacher and an individual child—is like having a conversation with a child (Jones & Courtney, 2002). Interviews offer teachers flexibility. A teacher can adapt the interview to meet whatever special needs a child has. Teachers, who really want to understand children's thinking, can ask the same question in different ways to uncover what children really know. Because the interview takes place face-to-face, the interviewer can quickly see when a child does not understand the question, and can rephrase or reword it (Seefeldt & Galper, 1998).

Interviews can take a number of forms. They can be entirely informal, open, or highly structured. Teachers of very young children can try to determine their understanding of a standard by asking open-ended questions such as "What can you tell me about . . . ?" Follow-up questions ask "How did you decide that?" "What might happen if . . . ?" "Why do you think . . . ?" Probing children's responses has been found to yield a great deal of information about children's knowledge or understanding of a concept. If children are not verbally articulate, teachers can change the question, asking the children to draw, dance, or show what they know about a given standard or benchmark.

Given the benchmark "children will develop understanding of the characteristics of organisms," teachers might structure an interview around the topic of children's concepts of seeds and their place in the plant growth cycle. Teachers might begin by saying to the child, "Tell me everything you know about seeds." Then they might proceed with questions such as "What will grow if you plant this corn seed?" "Will a flower grow?" Following Piagetian methodology, teachers might probe children's understanding with questions such as "A little girl told me that beans would grow from a corn seed: What do you think of that?" The point of the interview is to uncover children's thinking about the topic, not to obtain a correct answer.

More-structured interviews can be designed. These involve a set of questions that tap into children's understanding of a specific concept. Susan Gelman's (1995) research on children's concepts of life and death and of seeds and plants offer examples of structured interviews.

It takes skill and in-depth knowledge of both children and content to conduct an effective interview with young children. Interviewers also need to be objective and free from bias. Reliability and validity issues remain for using interviews for assessment, as they do for observations.

Task Performance

Another type of interview involves asking children to perform a task. The science, mathematics, and language and reading standards make use of task performance to assess children's attainment of benchmarks. If assessing children's attainment of language skills, then children can be asked to perform the skills. The mathematics benchmark "children will recognize, describe, extend, and create a wide variety of patterns" might be assessed by asking children to create their own pattern given a shoe string and wooden beads, copy a pattern, describe a pattern they made of wooden beads, or show which of a series of pictures is a pattern.

Performance tasks give children the opportunity to show what they know and can do, as well as use their imaginations and creativity. Nevertheless, asking children to perform a task shares the same problems and weaknesses of observations and interviews.

Work Sampling: Portfolios

Keeping samples of children's work is an established way of assessing young children's learning while in a preschool or primary setting. By sampling work at the beginning, middle, and end of a school year, teachers can make judgments about the progress of individual children. Children are not judged in relation to others, but in relation to their own growth, development, and learning. Meisels (1993), who developed the Work Sampling System, has demonstrated that portfolios, when they consist of a purposeful collection of children's work, provide a rich documentation of children's effort, progress, and achievement over a period of time.

Portfolios can be developed in a number of ways. In some classrooms teachers randomly select samples of work to include in each child's portfolio. Some teachers ask children to select products to be included in the portfolio. Meisels's Work Sampling System (1993) is more formal. It involves the identification and collection of two types of work: (1) core items and (2) other items. Core items are pieces of work sampled from the domains of personal and social development, language and literacy, mathematical thinking, scientific thinking, social studies, art and music, and physical development (Meisels, 1993). Items are dated, and a description of the goal, what the child did or said while completing the product, or other pertinent comments, are included. If items are to document attainment of a specific benchmark, then the benchmark is stated, and a judgment made about the level to which this product indicates attainment of the benchmark.

Portfolios are used in conferences with parents and children. Some teachers involve children in the discussion of the portfolio, with the children discussing different pieces of work, why and how they did these, and what they were thinking at the time. After a child has presented his or her work, then the teacher presents his or her point of view about the work. Discussion between families, children, and teachers then occur (Lawrence-Lightfoot, 2003).

Systematic portfolios have been found to be reliable indicators of children's achievement (Meisels, Liaw, Dorfman, & Nelson, 1995), and are popular with students, parents and teachers (Meisels, Xue, Bickel, Nicholson, & Atkins-Burnett, 2001). Lawrence-Lightfoot (2003) suggested that some of the best parent-teacher conferences she studied were those that involved children: Even children 5 or 6 years of age were able to present profound insights into their work, progress, and achievement.

Assessing children's achievement through the use of portfolios is highly congruent with benchmarks. Student achievement of procedural benchmarks typically revolves around children producing some product. These products then are dated, their goal or purpose identified, and they are filed in children's portfolios. For example, the history standards (NCHS, 1994) call for students to construct time lines; create narratives with beginnings, middles, and endings; develop picture time lines; and obtain information from the past, conduct interviews, and present their findings through illustrations or stories. Any or all of these, when a part of a child's portfolio, could offer evidence of the child's attainment of specific benchmarks.

Geography standards and benchmarks indicate that children are to draw or sketch maps, use labels and symbols to identify physical and human features of places, write a story or play about communities being cut off from others, write descriptions of places, and use photos and other visual materials to create a display to answer questions such as "Where do people live?" and "What kinds of jobs do they have?"

Procedural and contextual benchmarks are common to the science standards. These typically call for students to make the results of their investigations public. In doing so, children create written descriptions; construct displays; and draw, paint, or construct depictions of their investigations. Additionally, the science standards generally ask students to perform a task or demonstrate knowledge. Digital photos of children measuring, weighing, investigating what objects can do, planting seeds, and so on can be taken, dated, and described, and become valuable portfolio items.

CULTURAL APPROPRIATENESS AND CHILDREN WITH SPECIAL NEEDS

The very word *standard* calls up images of standardized children, each looking like the other, each dressed the same, each sitting still doing the same thing at the same time. Nothing could be further from the truth. The standards recognize children as dynamic individuals who learn through doing and whose learning is assessed through doing.

Nevertheless, the standards give very limited attention to children who may have special needs or to those who are new to our country. Teachers, when adapting standards and the benchmarks, will want to keep in mind the assessment of children who do have special needs.

The Early Childhood Research Institute on Culturally and Linguistically Appropriate Services (http://www.clas.uiuc.edu) suggests beginning with children's families. With translators, if necessary, teachers should meet with families new to our country. The goal would be to learn the families' preferred form of communica-

tion and any suggestions they have for people willing to work with the teachers and their children in class. Someone fluent in the language of the family would be helpful in interpreting observations or conducting interviews.

When assessment stems from the curriculum and involves children in actual doing, a measure of cultural relevance is assured. Santos (2004) suggests that the materials of the classroom, especially those used in assessing children's achievement of benchmarks, be reviewed to make certain these acknowledge diversity. The content, design, illustrations, and photos of the assessment materials should be analyzed for

- Diversity of family structure
- Inclusion of multigenerations
- Equally powerful roles for both boys and girls
- Presence of children with disabilities
- Unbiased portrayal of religions
- Inclusion of people from differing socioeconomic status

Involving families in the assessment process is recommended. First, the family member can serve to translate and interpret what children are doing and why, explaining the norms of their culture. Then too, involving family members in their children's achievement of benchmarks serves to inform families of their importance in the education of their children.

Families also need to be involved in the analyzing and reporting of the results. Teachers should determine what form of communication families prefer or what would be most useful to families. Some results could be written and then delivered orally. Other results might only be delivered orally. As noted earlier, involving children in conferencing with parents has been found to be highly productive (Lawrence-Lightfoot, 2003).

IN SUMMARY

- Standards declare content children are to know. Benchmarks state with specificity what students are to know and be able to do at a given level of development or schooling.
- Because benchmarks may be vague and describe what children are to know at a given point in time, teachers will have to judge benchmarks for their developmental appropriateness.
- Benchmarks cannot be assessed through standardized tests. Benchmarks call for assessment through observation, interviewing children, asking children to perform tasks, and collecting and analyzing work samples.

APPENDIX: NORMAL DEVELOPMENTAL MILESTONES FOR THREE- TO SIX-YEAR-OLDS

Three-Year-Olds

Self, social, and motivational development

- Do not describe themselves in terms of traits, but know their names, and when asked to tell about themselves, will talk about the toys they have or what these toys do
- Engage in predominately solitary and parallel play
- Show the beginning of independence
- Gain growing control over emotions
- Are egocentric in thought; treat others as objects or toys

Language and mathematics

- Achieve rapid growth in vocabulary, gaining an average of 2,000 words during the year
- Talk in monologue as if practicing language
- May have difficulty taking turns in conversation
- Can tell a simple story, but not in sequence, often forgetting the point of the story and focusing on favorite or remembered parts
- Know the difference between writing and drawing
- Can adapt their speech and style of nonverbal communication to listeners in culturally accepted ways, but need to be reminded of context (Bredekamp & Copple, 1997)
- Have intuitive ideas of numeracy, for example, most know the meaning of *more*
- Can distinguish one from many
- Know how old they are and how old they will be next year
- Have a sense of time, remember events, and have some sense of today and tomorrow
- Are unable to conserve number, matter, or quantity

Scientific inquiry and knowledge of the world

- Show preoperational thinking, bound to perception
- Abound in egocentric thinking, for example, "The moon follows me around"
- Express many "why" questions
- Attribute life (intent) to things that move (e.g., "The ball stopped because it was tired."), but know that machines are different from either animals or inanimate objects
- Are beginning the initial phases of inquiry, for example, will stack blocks to knock them down or roll crayons in their hands to find out what crayons can do

Large and fine motor skills

- Can walk, turn, and stop efficiently
- Are able to jump off low steps or objects
- Play actively and tire easily
- Can pour liquids, put large pegs in holes, build with blocks
- Can dress without assistance, but need help with buttons and so on
- Hold crayons with fingers instead of fist

Development in art and music

- Explore unfamiliar art materials, dumping markers or crayons on the table, rolling them around, or cutting snippets of paper just to find out how to use the scissors
- In the preschematic stage of art, produce uncontrolled scribbles in paint, crayon, and marker, documenting that the art of three-year-olds is partially a sensory motor activity
- May use both hands as they scribble
- Hold crayons, markers in a tight, overhand grip
- Develop rhythmic movements from large muscle, gross movements to specific and finer movements
- Enjoy chants, the foundation for singing
- Experiment with the idea of singing

Four-Year-Olds

Self, social, and motivational development

- Are moving from solitary to parallel play, sometimes engaging in give-and-take
- Show a growing sense of initiative and self-reliance
- Still describe themselves in terms of what they have or are doing, for example, "I'm building a fort"
- Can express emotions, for example, "I'm happy"
- Have occasional outbursts of anger that pass quickly
- Begin to try to please others, offering things to others, complimenting others
- Still have difficulty sharing, but are beginning to understand taking turns

Language and mathematics

- Increase their vocabulary by another 2,000 to 4,000 words, and learn new vocabulary quickly when directly related to their experiences
- Sometimes try to communicate more than their vocabulary allows, extending words to create new meaning, for example, "We piled all the stuff in the baby stroller, oh I mean the cart."
- Find taking turns in conversations difficult; can take turns, but they really want to talk about themselves and the things they do

- Are pushing the boundaries of language, enjoying the use of "bathroom" language for the fun of it, to shock as well as to test and learn what is culturally appropriate
- Have mastered nearly 90 percent of phonetics and syntax of language, but still overgeneralize verb tense, plurals, and pronouns
- Know the names of a few letters, recognize familiar logographics, and incorporate letters and pretend writing in their drawings and paintings
- Understand that words such as *one* and *two* stand for numbers and can represent the quantity of objects
- Can usually count by memory in sequence from one to ten
- Can identify some numerals, such as 4, their age
- Can perform simple number operations, for example, "You took one away, I need one more"
- Are still not capable of understanding conservation of number, quantity, or matter
- Are learning the names of simple shapes such as circle and square
- Can make comparisons, for example, "She has a bigger piece of cake than I do"

Scientific Inquiry and Knowledge of the World

- Continue in preoperational thinking, bound by perception
- Persist at a task, trying out different hypotheses until a solution is reached
- Learn quickly to use tools, for example, to reach objects
- Classify and make inferences about objects
- Give animistic answers to some questions, for example, "Why does the sun rise? Because I get up," and rational, mechanical answers to others, for example, "Why does a tire go flat? Because it got a hole in it"

Large and fine motor skills

- Build complex block structures
- Can string small beads and complete puzzles
- Use scissors and other tools
- Walk, run, and jump with skill
- Can engage in long periods of active play and exercise

Development in art and music

- Control scribbles, repeating circles, lines, and other forms
- Name their drawings or paintings after they have completed them
- Hold implements more like an adult
- Move to music with increased smoothness

- Discover joy and relaxation through listening to music
- When they sing, are directional in tone, their voices going either up or down
- Can learn songs that have repetition, echo, and also cumulative songs

Five- and Six-Year-Olds

Self, social, and motivational development

- Have a firmer sense of self
- Are refining gender roles, often with a tendency to stereotype
- Enjoy cooperative play with others, especially socio-dramatic play
- Cooperate and generally share well
- Use verbal insults or threaten to hit, but use less physical aggression
- Persist at tasks for longer periods
- Can plan out an activity and return to the same activity the next day

Language and mathematics

- Are continuing to expand their language growth, with a vocabulary of 5,000 to 8,000 words
- Increase their sentence length, and use more complex sentence structure
- Still overgeneralize rules, using *foots* instead of *feet* but correcting themselves when they do so
- Can retell stories in sequence
- Have favorite stories, recognize the work of familiar authors, compose stories themselves, and act out stories and poems
- Use nonverbal gestures to communicate ideas
- If in a bilingual environment, will begin to use familiar words in another language, for example, "*Rosa* is red in Spanish," Claire told her mother.
- Take turns in conversations, still interrupting to talk about themselves, but not as frequently
- Can count to 10 and through the teens; are interested in learning to write numerals; begin copying numbers
- Have a sense of time, but still mainly their own, knowing when events close to them take place
- Begin to learn to classify on the basis of one characteristic such as color or size, and can articulate why they place things together
- Can identify common shapes
- Are developing language of measurement, and both the concepts and language to express locations such as *under* and *over*, *in* and *out*
- Are still unable to conserve matter, number, and quantity

- Begin counting using one-to-one correspondence, placing one cup and one napkin at a place
- Perform simple number operations, taking away and adding objects to make more or less

Scientific inquiry and knowledge of the world

- Begin to question conservation of amount and length
- Benefit from language and experiences that provide opportunities to use methods of science
- Experiment and invent solutions to solve problems
- Understand a variety of cause-and-effect relations
- Form loosely held analogies, rather than coherent theories; explain the rain cycle as "raining up" and "raining down," not in terms of evaporation
- Have well-formed theories about physical objects

Large and fine motor skills

- Use tools, scissors, hammers, and drawing and painting tools with efficiency

- Assemble and disassemble objects
- Can walk backward, skip, balance on walking beam, hop, jump, and climb well
- Have high sustained physical energy

Development in art and music

- Are familiar with and able to use a wide variety of art materials
- Develop forms and schema to represent their world, for example, a circle with sticks extending from it is a mother, a circle and stick is a tree, and so on
- Produce schema that are fairly representational
- Make decisions about what they are drawing, painting, modeling, before they begin
- Recognize their work and the work of others
- Have voice range from middle C to middle B
- Correlate singing with a range of interests and skills

Source: *Pre-K Standards: Guidelines for Teaching and Learning*, by CTB/McGraw-Hill, 2002. (http://www.CTB.com)

PART III

IMPLEMENTING STANDARDS

CHAPTER 5

The Integrated Curriculum and Standards

Although standards define discrete content from separate subject areas children are to learn at a given time, the standards also form an integrated whole. Each of the separate subject matter content standards advocate integration. First, each of the subject matter content standards mandate integration within the discipline. Next, each advocates integration of subject matter content throughout the total curriculum. As a result, standards have the potential to become the foundation for integrated curricula.

The goals of this chapter are to

- Build a case for the relationship between the nature of children's learning and the integrated curriculum
- Present the barriers to integrating the curriculum
- Describe how the standards can foster and promote an integrated curriculum
- Begin illustrating a standards-based, integrated curriculum

CHILDREN'S LEARNING

Children are whole beings. They bring their entire, whole bodies to school, not just their heads. Just as children cannot be separated into body parts for learning, jumping and running, or socializing, they cannot be separated into parts for learning math, language, science, the arts, or anything else. John Dewey (1944) expressed it this way:

> The child's life is an integral, a total one. There is no conscious isolation, conscious distinction. The things that occupy him are held together by the unity of the personal and social interests which his life carries along. (p. 341)

Teachers who think children's learning can be separated from the rest of their bodies probably would adopt a program of direct instruction in which teachers are given a script—a plan of what teachers are to say and do, what children are to do, and how children are to be assessed.

Direct instruction generally involves children sitting in a group with the teacher talking to them. At times children are asked to repeat what the teacher has said or to respond to carefully scripted questions. Sometimes individual children are called upon to complete some task, with the rest looking on, perhaps counting marshmallows by 10s to represent the 100 days they have spent in school. Children nod their heads and recite what the teacher tells them to. Each separate subject matter is taught in turn. There is no attempt to integrate one subject with another.

This method of teaching separate subject matter through direct instruction seems simple. And it may be simple for teachers. After all, a great deal of thinking and planning has been done for them. All teachers need to do is follow the prescribed plans.

The problem is that young children's learning is based on their physical, social, and mental interactions with others and their environment (NCR, 2001b; Piaget, 1969; Vygotsky, 1986). Because children's learning comes from interactions with the world and others, teaching and learning is as whole as they are.

Children who bring their entire bodies to school do not learn by sitting still, listening to a teacher, and reciting what the teacher says. It is true that children, like parrots in a zoo, can learn to give the right answer to a question, once they have memorized it and learned it by rote. But when their knowledge of rote learning is probed—for instance, if you ask children who can count by rote to 100 which number, 40 or 70, is the largest—they will be puzzled, unsure of even what the question means.

Then too, direct instruction is limiting. It is limited to exactly what is to be taught and learned. Young children, however, want to know about stinkbugs, water, worms, hair, cheese. Driven by the need to know, to achieve mastery over self, others, and their world, young children are eager learners.

Learning is not a passive activity; rather it is an active, do-it-yourself experience. In order to learn, children need opportunities to explore, to observe details, to think about things. Teachers need to provide intellectually challenging learning experiences that give children the opportunity to figure out things for themselves, to make choices, and to take the initiative.

Young children's thinking is different from that of elementary school children or adults. Today, as in the past, young children's thinking is

- *Guided by their perception.* Containers that are taller than others are believed to hold more than containers that are shorter but wider. The largest person is thought to be the oldest. A group of candies spread out on a table is perceived as having more than the same number of candies piled together on the table.
- *Magical.* Reindeer that fly are not a problem for young children. If reindeer want to fly, then of course, they can.
- *Egocentric.* Children tend to believe that everyone thinks the same way they do. They do not under-

Young children do not learn by sitting still.

stand that someone can have a different belief about something.
- *Preoperational.* Children do not use the logical mental operations that older children and adults use to make sense of their experiences.

During the period of early childhood, from birth through age 8 or 9, astonishing changes take place in children's ability to think, reason, communicate, and consider the ideas of others. With experiences and with adult guidance and direction, children make great cognitive and academic gains.

To challenge their preoperational thinking, children's experiences with learning must be firsthand. Children need to handle, count, and count again to find out that they have the same number of blocks regardless of how they are arranged. Children need social interaction to challenge their thinking and consider the views of others. They need to argue. Holding a blanket, one may say, "This is my cape—I'm Supergirl." The other says, "I want that. It's my blankie for my baby." In solving the problem, both children will have the experience of thinking about their own thinking and considering the thinking of another.

Look into a first-grade classroom in one urban school for young children, and see what an integrated curriculum looks like:

A group of children is deeply engaged in building with blocks. They argue a bit and count the blocks they have and those they need. Then they consult a book on skyscrapers the teacher has placed in the block area book basket. Convinced that they are on the right track, the children continue their vertical building. Four children are busily painting away at the easels. Two are working together at a computer. All the other children are also busy doing things—playing board games, reading books together, creating a flannel board story, or putting finishing touches to an art project. As they do so, their thinking is continually being challenged. Throughout the room, the children are active—physically, socially, and mentally. They are thinking, identifying problems, and finding ways of solving them.

The teacher is active as well. She stops at the block area and discusses principles of balance and the need for a foundation for tall block buildings. She finds some heavy paper and markers for the children so they can make signs for their building. As she circulates through the room, the teacher stops to talk and work with individual children and small groups of children. She uses vocabulary new to children, offers facts

Children identify and solve problems when building with blocks.

or ideas that extend children's knowledge and thinking, asks children to count and use their knowledge of mathematics, and involves them in writing and reading.

An integrated curriculum does not negate individual or small-group instruction. After circulating through the room, the teacher sits at a small table and calls children to work with her on a shared reading project. Children read together, talk, and write about what they've read. She teaches phonic skills, "Look, here is the word family *an*, and this is the letter *f*, put the two together, and you have the word *fan*."

The integrated curriculum of this classroom is very different from that of direct instruction. In this classroom, separate goals and objectives are nested within an environment rich with learning opportunities that are socially relevant and responsive to the way children learn. Content from the arts, physical sciences, mathematics, and language learning and reading are integrated into a whole, rather than being presented to children as separate subjects.

BARRIERS TO AN INTEGRATED CURRICULUM

An integrated curriculum has long been advocated, not just for young children but for older students as well. Those believing that each individual child's learning is governed by his or her growth and development have long supported an integrated curriculum. These maturationists believe children's growth and learning is determined by a built-in genetic code. All children, according to maturation theories, develop, grow, and learn in the same predictable ways. The goal of education is to match what children are to learn to their development. For instance, you cannot teach a child to walk until the child is developmentally ready to walk. Nor can you teach a child to talk until the child is ready to talk. Therefore, the curriculum is guided by children's growth.

An integrated curriculum, the maturationists believe, has the potential to meet individual children's needs. Instead of a lockstep, sit-and-listen curriculum of direct instruction in separate subject areas, with all children expected to learn the same thing at the same time, an integrated curriculum allows children to move at their own pace. For example, children building with blocks are able to use their own ideas of mathematics as they build, and each has the opportunity to gain new and more complex ideas of math.

In addition to the maturationists, cognitive psychologists advocate for an integrated curriculum on the grounds that it offers children the opportunity to build or construct abstract ideas or concepts. Cognitive psychologists claim that what the brain does best is integrate—make connections that apply to problem solving. A separate subject curriculum denies the very nature of the function of the brain. According to these theories, cognition or thinking develops best when there is an active exchange between children and the environment, an environment in which "teachers initiate activities designed to foster children's reasoning and problem-solving abilities, interacting with children during child-designed activities to add new ideas or enhance learning" (NRC, 2001a, p. 139).

Reasoning and problem solving are central to an integrated curriculum. The curriculum is not prepackaged or prescribed, but rather embedded in children's firsthand interactions with their physical and social environments. This interaction gives them many opportunities for mental activity; it offers them the material necessary to formulate and refine problems, set goals, collect data from a variety of sources, and reach conclusions (NCTM, 2000).

Given the endorsements for the potential of an integrated curriculum to foster children's thinking and cognitive development, one might expect to find widespread use of an integrated curriculum throughout the nation's schools. This is not the case at all. In fact, it's difficult to find any integrated curricula in today's schools. A number of factors work against implementing integrated curriculum:

1. Conflicting educational theories
2. Differing teacher belief systems about how children learn
3. Difficulties for teachers in understanding, implementing, and assessing integrated curriculum
4. Physical and organizational characteristics of today's schools

Conflicting Theories

While cognitive psychologists and maturational theorists advocate an integrated curriculum on the grounds that it matches the way children grow and learn to think, other theories are politically and socially in favor today. The behavioral or empiricist theories are those that are strongly advocated in today's schools.

Behavioral theorists think of children's learning, not as a whole, but as consisting of separate pieces. They argue that the structure of the curriculum is the most important thing, not knowledge of the child's growth, development, or thinking skills. To enable learning anything—a fact, concept, how to do something, or even how to act—the teacher must begin by first breaking the task down and identifying the bits and pieces of the task. Then a teacher can present the task to the children, usually as a group, in hierarchical, sequential steps. When one step is mastered, children move on to master the next, until the whole is achieved. If a child does not master a step, it isn't the child's fault, but the fault of the curriculum, perhaps how the steps were sequenced or practiced. The teaching process is analyzed and revised, and the child is presented with the material until it is mastered.

While teachers following the empiricist or behavioral theories of learning might provide children with paper and markers to write signs for their block buildings, they would not think of this as a writing or reading activity. Instead, they would teach children the name of each letter of the alphabet in turn, and then after children know all the names and sounds of the letters and how to write them, would begin teaching reading.

The result of the behavioral theories is an academic curriculum of direct instruction in which children are presented with isolated skills to learn. Assessment is relatively easy. Children are asked to learn isolated skills, and all one has to do is assess these skills. Because children are directly taught the facts and skills that are going to be tested, children may be able to pass the test. The results of the assessment of children's achievement

of isolated skills and facts through direct instruction has impressed legislators, so politicians, who promise to improve the quality of public education, promote direct instruction. Direct instruction appeals to socially conservative people as well: Those who believe children need to be controlled and, like passive vessels, filled with knowledge find the characteristics of direct instruction appealing.

Differing Teacher Beliefs and Abilities

Teachers, like theorists, hold differing ideas of the curriculum. Teachers' beliefs about how children learn affect how curriculum is put into practice (Bredekamp & Rosegrant, 1997). If teachers are to implement an integrated curriculum, they must first believe that children are whole beings who learn through their interactions with the environment. But since many teachers were taught as children through direct instruction, the method is familiar and comfortable to them, and they likely choose to implement it in their classrooms.

Teachers may also be uncomfortable with their own abilities to implement an integrated curriculum. The challenges involved in planning and implementing an integrated curriculum are great. Teachers must be specialists in each separate subject matter area, as well as specialists in how children learn.

Assessment in an integrated curriculum is also much more complex than in direct instruction. Teachers must develop "assessment literacy" (NAEYC/NAECS/SDE, 2003); become skilled in conducting and using observations, documentation, forms of criterion- or performance-oriented assessment; and use broad, varied, and complementary methods of assessment for all children.

Characteristics of Schools

Teachers may find limited support from school systems in implementing an integrated curriculum. Unlike direct instruction, which only requires space for children and a teacher and few materials, only paper and markers, an integrated curriculum requires space, a different concept of time, and a variety of learning materials and experiences.

Generally, the physical characteristics of schools, their very structure in fact, hinder development of an integrated curriculum. Classrooms often are limited in space for children to work as individuals or with small groups. You need "stuff" to put an integrated curriculum into practice. Dewey (1944) called for more raw materials in schools. He believed that with raw materials—wood, sand, water, clay, paints, things to construct with, to pull apart and put together again—children's minds would be fully active.

A different way of thinking about time also is required to implement integrated curriculum. Children involved in a study of the properties of water, for example, need time to carry out experiments, try again, find resources, rethink their original ideas, and solve problems. The ways school days are structured, with time for recess, lunch, prescribed physical education, can limit a teacher's flexibility. See Figure 5.1 for a summary of what is required to implement an integrated curriculum.

STANDARDS INTEGRATE THE CURRICULUM

Standards specifically outline content children are to learn in a given subject area. For that reason standards could become another barrier to the implementation of an integrated curriculum. Quite the opposite, however, may be the case. The standards call for total integration of the curriculum. If standards are to have a lasting impact on the field of early education, it may be because of this focus on integration.

Standards can work in at least four ways to foster, rather than negate, the implementation of integrated curricula in schools for young children:

1. The authors and sponsors of the standards advocate for and support curriculum integration.
2. The overwhelming number of standards require greater organization and unification of the curriculum if they are to be implemented.
3. The identification of the big ideas in given subject area disciplines provide a clear framework for creating an integrated curriculum.

Figure 5.1. Prerequisites for an Integrated Curriculum

---

1. Teachers who
   • Believe children are whole beings whose learning is whole
   • Understand cognitive theories of how children think and learn
   • Utilize multiple instructional strategies for individual children as well as small and whole groups
   • Possess knowledge of the structure of each subject matter area
   • Develop skills in multiple methods of assessing children's growth, development, and learning

2. Administrators who think differently about time, space, and teaching

3. Physical environments that support firsthand learning

---

4. Teaching for thinking and problem solving is a common theme of nearly every set of standards from the separate subject areas.

Advocates for Integration

The authors of the standards advocate a unified, integrated curriculum. For example, the National Science Education Standards (NCR/NAS, 1996) present conceptual and procedural schemes that unify the science disciplines. These themes provide teachers with powerful ideas to help them understand the natural and human-made world. Additionally, the authors of the science standards call for integration of the total curriculum and assessment.

The topic of sound, for example, was taught to third graders through a unit on music. To conclude the study of sound, the teacher collected a variety of materials, including boxes, tubes, rubber, string, wire, and so on. She asked children, while working with a group, to construct musical instruments. Children had to work together, talking and arguing as they collaborated to create instruments. Experts—several sixth graders—were asked to consult with the third graders. Resource books were available. At the end of the second week children's work was assessed. Each child played his or her instrument for the group. They had to demonstrate how the instrument made a sound, how they could make the sound loud or soft, higher or lower, and explain how they had made the instrument.

Curriculum and Evaluation Standards for School Mathematics (NCTM, 1989) presents standards for mathematical learning, not as separate subject matter topics, but as carefully interwoven strands designed to support the learning of connected mathematical ideas. These standards call for a curriculum that encourages children to explore mathematical ideas in the context of "real-world experiences" (p. 16). An assumption is that children will have extensive and thoughtful use of physical materials including buttons, beans, shells, egg cartons, rulers, cubes, tiles, pattern blocks, and much more. The math standards strive to integrate mathematics into children's everyday life. "Only through extended exposure to integrated topics will children have a better chance of retaining the concepts and skills they are taught" (p. 33). To incorporate measurement into daily activities, children could measure which of their block buildings is the tallest and how tall it is; how far they can go in three, four, or more jumps; and so on.

The National Standards for History, for Grades K–4 view the study of history as a highly integrative study (see Figure 5.2). While exploring the past, children will also be studying the geographical places in which people lived and the events that took place. The oral traditions, art, music, and architecture, as well as the

Figure 5.2. Integrating History into the Curriculum

The history standards incorporate content from other disciplines.

Geography

Making and using maps

Visual Arts

Drawing, painting, or otherwise representing ideas of history

Music

Studying culture by enjoying music from a variety of cultures

Language and Literacy

Adopting a literature-centered approach to history

Mathematics

Creating graphs to represent information

Science and Technology

Studying technology and its effects

---

laws and institutions people lived by, will be studied as well. "In short, studies in history necessarily include geographic, economic, political, and scientific study" (NCHS, 1996, p. 13).

Literature, as a tool for teaching history, is strongly encouraged throughout the history standards. "Lessons in literature can include literacy selections from historical fiction, biography, and other readings important to the history curriculum as well as to the language arts" (NCHS, 1996, p. 13). Creative thinking is encouraged as children are asked to create group stories in history, and language and literacy skills are promoted as children write their own historical narratives, letters, and journals.

The National Standards for Arts Education are based on the principle that standards help children make connections between concepts and across subjects. Arts educators claim that one of the things the arts do best is forge connections not just between the various disciplines comprising the arts—dance, the visual arts, music, and theatre—but between and among other subject areas as well. "Connections among the arts or between the arts and other subjects are fundamental" (CNAEA, 1994, p. 13).

One critical way the arts are integral to the curriculum is the fact that any of the arts—music, the visual arts, dance, and theatre—are intellectual activities. When chil-

dren participate in the arts, they are forced to think. Creating or using any of the arts demands problem solving, reflection, analysis, synthesizing, and evaluation.

The arts bring multiculturalism to every classroom. Throughout time, every culture has been defined by the arts. As children sing Spanish songs, listen to music from the Far East, or study patterns found on pottery created during different times and in different cultures, they gain an idea of the universals of human culture. All cultures create and use the arts. The form the arts take reflects the values, beliefs, dreams, myths, and resources of that culture.

The arts standards describe how the arts are correlated with subject matter disciplines as well as integrated. The musical arts are filled with mathematical concepts. Music requires thinking about intervals, counting, making and finding patterns, all of which are content from the mathematics standards. Music and mathematics then are correlated with each other. They stand side by side.

The Overwhelming Number of Standards

"What's a teacher to do?" asks a kindergarten teacher. "I have a book of standards from the state department of education, another from the math and science associations, and then another bunch of standards on reading and writing. You tell me how anyone, anywhere, could implement every one of these standards. It's impossible."

True. It would be impossible to address each and every standard separately. The characteristics of standards would make it impossible for any one group of children to learn all of the information required in any one set of standards, much less all of them. Pick up any set of standards. Whether looking at mathematics, reading, geography, or science standards, you will find yourself overwhelmed with the number of concepts, skills, and outcomes children are to achieve.

It would be impossible to accomplish the goals of even one set of standards if standards are thought of as separate subject matter entities rather than a part of an integrated whole. Incorporating standards into an integrated curriculum offers the only feasible solution to working with standards. Consequently, the standards have the potential to integrate the curriculum.

Figure 5.3 provides an example of the variety of standards that can be addressed through block building. Obviously, spending one morning building with blocks is not enough if children are to form complex concepts from the disciplines of mathematics, language, or technology. Learning is a gradual process. When standards are a part of an integrated curriculum, children have the opportunity to experience the same concept in a variety of ways. Each new experience with the

Figure 5.3. Standards and Block Building

Mathematics

Counting blocks—develop number sense

Creating patterns—recognize, describe, extend, and create a wide variety of patterns

Identifying shapes—develop spatial senses

Geography

Recognizing location—describe the position of an object by relating it to another object or the background

Science

Experiencing gravity—understand that gravity is the force that holds us to the earth's surface

Technology

Constructing and creating—work together in teams with individuals doing different things that contribute to the results

Language and Literacy

Making signs—inform others through writing, vocabulary, and word choices, emergent spelling

Observant teachers would no doubt have added other standards to this list, perhaps noting the vocabulary children used, the nature of child/child interactions, and concepts from the physical sciences that were being utilized during block building.

---

concept forces children to rethink their existing ideas, assimilating and accommodating this additional information to form a better, more accurate way of thinking.

The Big Ideas: Identification of Key Concepts

The standards also have the potential to promote integrated curricula because they clearly define, delineate, and explain the structure of knowledge or the content children are to learn in a given subject area. This is what Bruner (1966) called for when he wrote *Toward a Theory of Instruction.* His idea was that if the big ideas, or concepts key to a given subject matter discipline, could be identified, these ideas would form the foundation for the curriculum.

Bruner's ideas, while well-received, were not widely implemented. The problem was that in 1966 the structure, or the big ideas, of each subject matter discipline had not been fully identified or delineated. With the advent of the standards, however, teachers and curriculum developers now have a clear idea of the structure of content in each subject matter. Knowledge of standards helps teachers delineate content and build a coherent and meaningful curriculum that continues through children's early educational experiences.

Standards delineate content. The structure of the standards enables teachers to know the embryonic or initial concepts children are to learn in order to move onto mastering the next, more advanced, conventional, and complex concepts. This knowledge gives teachers the tools they need to plan a whole, integrated, and meaningful curriculum for young children.

Before the advent of standards, teachers were more or less left on their own to decide what content children were to learn. This led to a curriculum that was more scattered than coherent. Content was often chosen in a hit or miss fashion. The result was a sampling of knowledge from a sampling of discipline areas.

Standards provide for a continuous curriculum. A problem facing early childhood education is that of curriculum continuity. Early education is governed by a variety of agencies. The federal government sponsors some programs such as Head Start; others are church related, or run privately. Still other early education programs are governed by states or school systems.

Since programs are uncoordinated, there has been no continuity of curriculum. Children might study butterflies one year, and repeat the same unit the next year in a different program. Attempts were made in the past to provide for continuity of curriculum within programs, so that as children moved from one to another, progress would be made. These, however, were not successful because the structure of content was not available. With standards identifying what children can and should be learning at differing ages, programs, even under differing auspices, will be able to build a continuous, coherent curriculum.

Standards promote meaning. With knowledge of content, teachers can design curriculum with integrity and meaning. The comparison that follows can illustrate how standards foster meaningful curriculum.

Two teachers of four-year-olds took their classes on a spring walk with the goal of observing cherry trees in bloom. One teacher sang marching songs along the walk, stopping for the children to play under the blooming trees.

The other teacher read over the science standards prior to the experience. Along the way she focused the children's observations. She asked them to feel the bark of the cherry tree and to find out where the branches grew from the trunk. The children looked at cherry blossoms through magnifying glasses. The teacher named the petals and stamen. The children counted the petals. Cherry blossoms were compared to forsythia blossoms. And yes, the children did run around and play under the cherry trees.

When both groups of children were asked what they had learned at school that day, the children in the first group said, "We went on a walk." Children in the other group said, "Cherry blossoms have five petals," "Bark is rough," "All blossoms have a stamen," "Some blossoms are pink and some are yellow," "Branches grow from trunks," and "cherries grow from cherry blossoms."

Emphasis on Thinking and Problem Solving

Essential to the health of a democratic society are citizens who can think, identify problems, and then find creative ways to solve them. For a democratic society to survive, its citizens must be able to not only maintain that society but also improve on it.

Knowledge of isolated facts, while necessary for thinking and solving problems, is not enough. Authors of standards recognize this and have made thinking and problem solving central to the standards. At the core of standards for mathematics, science, the arts, literacy, history, geography, and the other social sciences are the thinking processes of inquiry or problem solving (see Figure 5.4).

Figure 5.4. Thinking and Problem-Solving Skills

- *Observing*—being able to focus attention; looking and looking again; examining an object, event, or situation from different angles

- *Questioning*—being able to sense a problem and ask meaningful questions

- *Locating, finding and collecting information*—measuring and weighing; finding out what will happen; learning from experts; books, and other resources

- *Analyzing information*—comparing, contrasting, asking more questions, and organizing the information collected

- *Reaching conclusions*—seeing relationships, generalizing, reaching and reflecting on conclusions

---

One-third of the National Science Education Standards (NCR/NAS, 1996) are based on principles of thinking. "Scientific literacy means that a person can ask, find, or determine answers to questions" (p. 22). These standards are based on the idea that children will learn to observe, question, identify problems, collect information, analyze that information, and reach solutions.

The central focus of the mathematics standards is problem solving. Problem solving is "a primary goal of all mathematics instruction and an integral part of all mathematical activity. Problem solving is not a distinct topic but a process that should permeate the entire program and provide the context in which concepts and skills can be learned" (NCTM, 1989, p. 83).

Reading and Writing Grade by Grade: Primary Literacy Standards (New Standards, 1999) takes the position that reading is a problem-solving, thinking process. "Reading is a complex skill that involves strategies for puzzling out meaning and gauging understanding. The ultimate goal of reading is getting the meaning" (p. 19).

Historians maintain that thinking skills cannot be separated from historical content. Thinking does not occur in a vacuum; rather, each thinking skill—observing, asking questions, locating and collecting information, analyzing data, and reaching conclusions—requires content (NCHS, 1996). In other words, children need something to think about—content.

Geographers believe it is essential for students to develop thinking skills that will enable them to "observe patterns, associations, and spatial order" (GESP, 1994, p. 45). Children, the geographers claim, need to develop critical thinking skills beyond those that are unique to geography. The generic thinking processes of knowing, inferring, analyzing, judging, hypothesizing, generalizing, predicting, and making decisions, which are necessary for the study of geography, are equally as important in every other field.

The Consortium of National Arts Education Associations (1994) states that education in the arts is necessary, not only because the arts cultivate the whole child, but because the arts require an active mind. By participating in the arts, children are initiated into a new way of perceiving and thinking. Through the arts children learn to observe, solve problems, imagine, create, and reflect. The powerful thinking skills of analyzing, synthesizing, and evaluating are a part of music, dance, the visual arts, and the theatre.

UNITS, THEMES, AND PROJECTS

How do you achieve a whole unified curriculum, one that integrates content from each subject area discipline and teaches children complex thinking skills? A whole, unified curriculum is best achieved through unit, thematic, or project learning (see Figure 5.5).

Units, thematic learning, and the project approach all have their roots in the philosophy of John Dewey (1944). Based on Dewey's ideas of whole learning, teachers developed units to organize the curriculum. These early units were more or less teacher directed (M. Hughes, 1934), but did demonstrate how the curriculum could be planned and implemented as a complete whole.

In the 1960s the philosophies of Piaget, Vygotsky, Bruner, and other cognitive psychologists gave support to the idea that curriculum should be whole and integrated. As pointed out earlier in this chapter, cognitive psychologists believe children are active learners, constructing knowledge through their own mental, physical, and social activity. This belief led to more child involvement in planning and implementing learning, and instead of units, teachers began to use thematic learning. Without the total structure of a unit plan, children as well as teachers guide thematic learning experiences. Some themes last a day or two, others an entire year.

An example of a theme that lasted a couple of days was the study of worms. Following a heavy rain, children in one child care center became enthralled with the number of worms on the sidewalk. They looked for eyes and legs, watched the worms move, and marveled at how a worm could stretch itself out and then become shorter again.

Back inside, the teacher and children pored over books about worms. Picking up on children's interest in worms, the teacher began planning a study of worms. The next day during morning meeting the teacher, showing children a large poster of worms and where they live, asked children what they wanted to learn about worms. They yawned, giggled, squirmed, and looked blank. Not wanting to abandon what seemed like a promising study, the teacher tried to introduce the topic of worms to the children the next day. Again, no amount of prompting was successful in sparking children's interests in worms and the teacher put her plans aside.

In the same classroom a study of wool lasted nearly the entire school year. One of the children's families raised sheep, spun wool, and sold yarn around the world. The class visited the farm to observe sheep. Children's interests led them to watching sheep being sheared and learning how to spin and dye wool, and how to knit. At the end of the year a book about sheep was written, copied, and sent home with each child.

Today the project approach to integrating the curriculum is popular. Projects are in-depth investigations undertaken by individual children or an entire group (Helm & Katz, 2001). The key feature of a project is that it is centered on thinking and problem-solving skills. The project is deliberately focused around finding answers to questions asked by children (Helm & Beneke, 2003).

The beginning of a project, Children Study Their Play Yard, is presented at the end of this chapter as an example of how the integration of standards can result in meaningful learning. The description of the project is continued at the ends of Chapters 6–10.

IN SUMMARY

- Standards, because they call for integration, have the potential to promote integrated teaching.
- Children are whole beings who learn through a whole, integrated curriculum.
- Barriers to implementing integrated curriculum include conflicting theories and ideas of curriculum, teachers' understanding and ability to implement integrated curriculum, and the characteristics of schools.
- Standards are best implemented through unit, project, or thematic learning that involves children in active investigations of their world.

SAMPLE INVESTIGATION: CHILDREN STUDY THEIR PLAY YARD

A major goal of project learning is to meet children's individual interests and needs as well as program goals. You know the children you teach so your planning and implementation of a similar project may differ from the suggested ideas that follow, which show how standards can be integrated through children studying their play yard.

Figure 5.5. Units, Thematic Learning, and Projects

- A curriculum that is unified and integrated around a topic or theme

- Experiential learning centered in children's here-and-now world

- Active engagement in thinking and problem solving, using the skills of observing, questioning, collecting and analyzing data, and reaching conclusions

- Reflection—reflecting on conclusions through drawing, writing, building, singing, dancing, constructing, or acting

CHOOSING A TOPIC

Study of the children's play yard meets the following criteria for topic selection. This investigation

- *Is of high interest to children.* Children love playing out of doors. They experience life to the fullest out of doors; they can run and shout, and stop and explore their natural and physical worlds.
- *Provides a common experience for children.* All children use and love their play yard. Here they have experiences in common, experiences that they can study and talk about, and thus learn that others have thoughts that may differ from theirs.
- *Can be studied firsthand.* Just stepping outside, children have multiple opportunities to observe, question, examine, measure, explore, and experiment.
- *Offers opportunities for children to initiate their own projects.* There is much to study on the play yard—the equipment, plant and animal life, motion, energy, the children themselves—any one of these could spark a "catalytic event" (Helm & Katz, 2001, p. 13) that would lead to the initiation of a project or become the theme for children's learning.
- *Can be standards based.* Standards from the content disciplines of science, the arts, language and literacy, mathematics, and social studies can be visited through study of the play yard.

SELECTING STANDARDS

Meaningful learning can be standards based. Selected standards can serve to guide teachers in planning and implementing learning experiences through study of the play yard.

To select standards, teachers will need to review existing standards, the goals of their program, and the goals and objectives they hold for each child and the total group of children. For the study of the play yard, the following standards were selected and adapted to different age groups:

Scientific inquiry—life sciences

Observe objects and living things.
Investigate life processes.
Develop and record conclusions.

The visual arts

Master a variety of art media.
Express ideas through the visual arts.
Recognize and talk about the concepts of art.

Language and literacy

Practice listening and speaking skills.
Develop vocabulary, including naming objects (nouns) and motions (verbs).
Engage in drawing and writing activities.

Mathematics

Develop concepts of counting.
Compare objects by size.
Make and use measurements in problem solving and everyday situations.

Geography

Develop knowledge of different earth surfaces and how the differences affect activities.
Make and use maps.

How these standards are translated into goals for children's learning and implemented will be illustrated through a study by children of their play yard. The investigation can begin as described below. At the ends of Chapters 6–10, activities to relate the investigation to specific content areas are suggested. The ideas are grouped by age. Standards, however, can be adapted to match any age child or developmental level.

ASSESSING AND DOCUMENTING CHILDREN'S LEARNING

Achievement of the standards is documented through authentic assessment techniques. By observing, interviewing, asking children to perform a task, and collecting and analyzing samples of children's work, teachers document and assess children's learning.

Teachers should remember, however, that children learn through repeated experiences. Children will need to visit the content identified in the standards frequently, in different situations, and through many and varied experiences, if they are to develop more conventional, complete, and accurate understanding of the world in which they live. For each of the parts of the play yard study described at the ends of Chapters 6–10, there will be examples of how children's learning of the integrated content identified in the standards could be evaluated through authentic assessment techniques.

BEGINNING THE INVESTIGATION

Units, thematic learning, and projects can be initiated by a "catalytic event," by children's questions and interests, or by teachers, based on their knowledge of children's interests and needs.

Toddlers (Two–Three Years Old)

Toddlers, who are just learning who they are and what they can do, need a light touch. Teachers of toddlers might:

- Informally ask individual children to think about what they'll do when they go out to play.
- Use spontaneous teachable moments as children are playing outside to introduce study of the play yard. One teacher asked a small group of children to find and name all the pieces of equipment on the play yard that were used for climbing. This simple beginning can lead to a full study of the play yard.

Preschoolers (Three–Four Years Old)

Preschoolers are better able to work together as a group. They also are able to gain meaning from songs and poems. Teachers of preschoolers might begin the theme by

- Singing a song such as "When We Go Out to Play," a North Carolina version of an old song, "On Our Holiday":
    What shall we do when we all go out, we all go out, we all go out?
    What shall we do when we all go out, when we all go out to play?
- Adding verses using children's ideas:
    We will . . . climb on the jungle gym; run and run; play in the sand; ride our bikes
- Chanting the poem "The Swing" (Stevenson, 1923) that begins "How do you like to go up in the swing, up in the swing so high?"

Kindergarten Children (Four–Five Years Old)

Kindergarten children are beginning to take meaning from symbols. Reading stories about the play yard

"We will climb on the jungle gym. . . ."

could be used to stimulate discussion and then study of the play yard.

- Introduce the study at a group meeting. To find out what children already know about the play yard ask:
    What do you know about our play yard?
    What is on our play yard?
    What do you like best about the play yard?
- Document children's ideas by making a list of what the children already *know*, and what they *want to know* about their play yard.

CHAPTER 6

Integrating the Science Standards

The science standards offer teachers a framework on which to build a meaningful, integrated science curriculum. The standards can provide teachers who are new to teaching science, as well as those who are well trained in science, with an understanding of appropriate science content for young children.

The science standards identify the big ideas of science. Knowledge of the big ideas of science enables teachers to focus and support children's scientific inquiries. With this knowledge teachers can design experiences that will challenge children's scientific thinking, enabling them to construct more conventional ways of scientific thinking.

The goals of this chapter are to

- Present the science standards
- Describe the processes of inquiry and how to foster the development of inquiry skills
- Illustrate how inquiry leads to gaining the knowledge described in the physical, life, and technology standards

THE SCIENCE STANDARDS

The science inquiry and science content standards that follow should be considered as examples of those that may be presented to teachers. These standards are based on *National Science Education Standards: Observe, Internet, Change, Learn* (NCR/NAS, 1996). Since those standards were developed for kindergarten through Grade 12, examples of how to implement the science standards in this chapter were derived from the Pre-K Standards of CTB/McGraw-Hill (2002) and McREL's *Content Knowledge: A Compendium of Standards and Benchmarks for K–12 Education* (Kendall & Marzano, 2004).

The scientific inquiry standards identify the processes of science education. The standards for the physical and life sciences and for technology describe or declare the content knowledge children are to learn.

1. Scientific inquiry
   1.a. Observing.
   1.b. Questioning.
   1.c. Investigating.
   1.d. Analyzing.
   1.e. Reaching conclusions.
   1.f. Communicating results to others.
2. The physical sciences
   2.a. Objects have many observable properties, including size, weight, shape, color, temperature, and the ability to react with other substances.
   2.b. Properties can be measured using tools, such as rulers, balances, and thermometers.
   2.c. Materials can exist in several states.
   2.d. Objects are made of one or more materials. Objects can be described by the properties of the materials from which they are made.
3. The life sciences
   3.a. Living organisms have basic needs.
   3.b. Each plant or animal has different structures that serve different functions in growth, survival, and reproduction.
   3.c. The behavior of individual organisms is influenced by interior and external cues.
   3.d. Plants and animals have life cycles.
   3.e. Characteristics of an organism are inherited from the parents of the organism.
4. Technology
   4.a. Some objects occur in nature; others have been designed and made by people to solve human problems.
   4.b. People create, invent, and design tools and techniques to solve problems.
   4.c. Tools help scientists make better observations, measurements, and equipment for investigations.

SCIENTIFIC INQUIRY

According to the standards, scientific inquiry means two things. First, inquiry is what scientists do. When scientists study the world, they observe, ask questions, and study their findings—analyzing, comparing, organizing, and contrasting—in order to reach conclusions. The scientific process is not complete until scientists communicate their findings and conclusions, and discuss these with others.

Inquiry also refers to the skills children are to develop and the activities they engage in as they develop scientific ideas and knowledge (NCR/NAS, 1996). These are the same skills scientists use. Children learn to observe, question, investigate, analyze the information collected, and finally reach conclusions. Children, like scientists, are finding problems, determining how to solve them, and reaching conclusions.

Scientific-inquiry skills are thinking skills. Dewey (1944) described the process of thinking as a process of mental engagement that required reflection. This process always begins with identifying a problem and ends with reflecting on the problem and its solution, and being able to communicate the process and solution to others.

Observing

The science standards indicate that during the period of early childhood, students' investigations are largely based on systematic observations of their world (NCR/NAS, 1996). Children are to learn, through systematic observation, the physical properties of objects and materials in their world, the position and motion of objects, as well as characteristics of organisms, their life cycles, and how organisms and environments interact.

Scientific skills are thinking skills.

As humans, we are constantly observing. Our observing is informal and unfocused, however. Scientists focus their observations in order to find out, to solve problems, or to increase their understanding. Children can be taught to do the same. To foster children's observation skills, teachers model observing, offer tools, scaffold children's skills, and provide practice.

Model observing. After a heavy rain earthworms seemed to cover a walk on the play yard. The children started smashing the worms with their feet. The teacher stopped them, asking them to look at the worms. "I wonder if they have legs" she said as she knelt down to look carefully at a worm. "After all, they are moving from place to place." Modeling her, the children too began to carefully look for legs. "They don't got legs," said one boy, "but they gots to have eyes to see the sidewalk." More observations took place.

Offer tools. Seeing children's interest in observing the worms, the teacher brought out plastic magnifying glasses so children could observe the worms more closely. "No," said, one child, "I don't see no eyes." Arguments ensued, causing more systematic observing as the teacher gently lifted one worm onto a piece of white paper for a focused observation.

Teachers can give children "viewing tubes" to help them focus their observations. Viewing tubes are made of discarded cardboard rolls from paper towels or toilet paper. Tubes can be covered with shiny contact paper, but nothing that could fall in children's eyes or hurt them in any way can be used to cover the tubes. Then too, tubes must either be disinfected after each use, or discarded and replaced with clean new ones (Seefeldt, 2004).

Provide scaffolding. Inquiring involves active thinking on the part of children and the teacher. Rather than letting children explore on their own and hoping they discover a scientific principle, teachers should actively scaffold, or support, children's learning.

"Watch this worm crawl," said the teacher. "Do you see legs? How many parts do you see? Let's look at some other worms and find out."

"Well," one child still insisted, "they still got to have eyes, everyone has eyes."

"I know what we'll do," responded the teacher, "we'll get some books on worms and find out how they move and see." (See Figure 6.1 for one class's observations on worms.)

Provide practice. In connection with their investigations of the world, children are frequently asked to focus their observations. Teachers might use these questions:

Figure 6.1. Recording Class Observations

Worms, Worms, Worms

We found worms on the sidewalk.
They do not have eyes.
They do not have legs.
They worm and squirm all around.

[*Experience story dictated by children in the Red Room*]

What is it like?
How does it move?
Are any of its parts symmetrical?
How would you describe its shape?
How are the leaves arranged on the branch?
Does it shine, reflect, or appear dull, or is it transparent?

Because observing involves senses other than that of looking, children are asked to observe also by listening.

Does it make a sound?
Listen, how many sounds do you hear?
How can you describe the sounds?
Why is it making a sound?
Which body part is making the sound?
How many sounds can you make?
What sounds do you hear at night?

Take caution. Teachers must take caution when asking children to use the other senses of feeling, smelling, and tasting as tools for observing. Young children should *not* be encouraged to feel, taste, or smell anything without an adult present. Without adult guidance, young children can easily be harmed, or even poisoned.

Questioning

Scientific discovery begins with a question. "How can we cure cancer?" "What strains of flu should be included in this year's flu vaccine?" Key to the processes of thinking, inquiry, and problem solving, the process of questioning is central to the science standards. Being able to ask questions about any specific content takes skill, knowledge, and security. To frame a good question requires at least tangential knowledge of content. For example, when a statistics teacher ends the first lecture asking, "Are there any questions?" are most students able to formulate an articulate question? Generally humans are unable to ask questions when they know little about a subject area or are too confused with a multitude of information.

In addition, children may have a question but not the skills to articulate what they really want to know. Children ask questions all the time. Sometimes children ask questions without really expecting or wanting an answer. It's as if hearing the question solves the problem for them. Other times children are unable to find the words or way of expressing their actual concerns. "Will I all come out?" a child asks his mother who is putting a bandage on a superficial cut. The child asks again, and again, and is told the bandage won't come off. What the child really wanted to know is if he would somehow escape or come out through the cut.

Then too, it takes psychological safety to ask a question. If people think others will laugh at them because they're asking something everyone else already knows, or if they are afraid others will think they're ignorant by asking a question, they will not ask the question. In some cultures and in some situations, it is considered rude to ask questions of authorities, such as teachers.

Sometimes children seem to ask too many questions: "Why is the sky blue?" "Why is the rain wet?" The goal of the standards related to questioning, however, is to foster children's ability to ask questions that can be answered through their observations and investigations in combination with scientific, conventional knowledge (see Figure 6.2 for assessing children's development in asking questions). To foster children's questioning skills teachers model questioning and provide materials and psychological safety (Rodd, 1999).

Model questioning. An open, questioning mind is modeled by teachers. When they question—"Why did this happen?" "What should we do now?" "I wonder why . . ."—teachers serve as models for children. And as the goal is to teach children to ask questions that can be answered through their own investigations (NCR/

Scientific skills involve learning to question.

Figure 6.2. Assessing Questioning

Observe children individually and as a group.

- During group meeting, which children are most likely to ask questions?
- Which children ask questions when working by themselves or in small groups?
- Are these the same children who question when in a large group?
- Are children asking questions to clarify their own thinking?
- Are children moving from asking questions without waiting for an answer, or do they wait for the answer, comment on it, or ask another question?

Record the questions over time and reflect on the characteristics of children's questions.

NAS, 1996), teachers follow through, finding ways for children to answer the questions.

"Why did this happen?" a teacher asked block builders who were confronted with buildings that collapsed. "We don't know," one of the children whined, "they just keep falling down." The teacher worked with the children as they built, asking what would happen if they put a block here or there, or paid attention to balance as they built.

Teachers' questions need to be thoughtful, carefully planned with specific purposes in mind (Epstein, 2003). If teachers mindlessly question everything, children will not learn to question with purpose and intent.

Provide materials. Materials that foster cause and effect or trial and error, that force children to experiment with causality, support questioning (Segatti, Brown-DuPaul, & Keyes, 2003). Battery-powered toys, pencil sharpeners that children turn, bubble-blowing materials, old-fashioned windup alarm clocks, kitchen timers, and the like present children with surprise.

Raw materials are necessary. When presented with wood, sand, art materials, and materials without a predetermined goal, children are forced to question: "What is this? What can I do with it? How can I do it?"

In addition to raw materials, teachers structure centers that require questioning. A cocoon found on the play yard and placed in a terrarium leads children to questioning and predicting what is inside the cocoon: "How do we care for it? When will the moth or butterfly emerge? What will it look like?"

Provide psychological safety. Psychological safety is necessary in order to be able to develop, articulate,

and ask questions. To build psychological safety, teachers make certain that

- *Children are in fact physically and psychologically safe.* No child is ever ridiculed or embarrassed, and no child is overwhelmed by the power of others. Discipline is consistent and firm, but not based on force or coercion.
- *Control is shared.* Teachers do not give orders and expect children to follow blindly (Seefeldt, 2005). Rather children are asked to make choices about what they will do and with whom, and decide when they have finished.
- *Freedom of thought and speech are fostered.* Children are expected to have opinions and their opinions are asked for and respected.

Investigating

Scientists investigate. They advance a theory or have an idea, and they try it out. If their idea fails, they try it another way. Children are like scientists in many ways. Perhaps they are born to be scientists. Instinctively, from the moment of birth, children engage in conducting investigations (NCR, 2001b).

Their first investigations of their world are natural. Children observe, listen, feel, taste, take apart, and explore everything in their environment (Humphreys, 2000). In an early childhood program children's inherent needs to find out about their world are refined and extended. Children are engaged in scientific investigations. They are taught the manipulative skills of measuring, cutting, connecting, switching, turning on and off, holding, pouring, tying, hooking, and so on (NCR/ NAS, 1996). Procedural skills develop as children learn to use beam balances; measure weight, force, or time; and use microscopes to observe the finer details of plants, animals, sand, or human-made materials (NCR/ NAS, 1996).

To foster scientific investigations, teachers provide children with tools for inquiry, and plan and implement fieldwork.

Provide tools for scientific inquiry. Scientific investigations require scientific equipment and tools. A science table might be equipped with a balance scale, digital scale, and hanging scale along with objects to weigh and compare, such as nuts and bolts, different types and sizes of pinecones, or blocks of wood. On another day the table may hold linear measuring tools. A tape measure, yard stick, unit cubes, and rulers might be featured, along with things to measure: material, wood, and toys.

Tools for scientific inquiry are located throughout the room. Containers and tools for measuring liquids

Tools are provided so children can study their world.

and sand are found on the water and sand table, along with the scales. The housekeeping area has kitchen timers, measuring cups and spoons, an indoor-outdoor thermometer, and other household measuring tools.

Plan and implement fieldwork. Equipped with tools, children begin investigating their world. The fields for investigation are those closest at hand—the classrooms, buildings, and play yards. As children mature and develop skills of investigating, fieldwork can extend to the neighborhood and into the broader community.

The goal or purpose could stem from a question children have, children's interests, or a program goal or objective. The goal could be as simple as taking a walk to look at a neighbor's flowers, going to the school office to find out what machines are used or who works in the office, walking up the stairs to the second floor to find out what happens upstairs, or going outside to find out how many pieces of play yard equipment are on the play yard. After children are familiar with fieldwork in and around their school, trips to local businesses, the post office, police or fire station, or other area of interest can take place.

The teacher must be certain the children know where they are going and why. One group of 5-year-olds were getting ready to visit the school's cafeteria. An observer asked the children "Where are you going?" The children replied, "On a field trip." Repeating the question several times, and in a number of ways, the children still insisted they were going on a "field trip." After they returned from their visit to the cafeteria, children were asked, "Where did you go?" Their reply was, "On a field trip." When questioned about what they saw, learned, or thought about the cafeteria, the children still talked about going on a trip.

Teachers can make the purpose of a trip clear by preparing the children. This teacher might have asked children who prepares their lunches, or what they know about the cafeteria. Perhaps an initial trip just to look at the cafeteria might have taken place to familiarize children with the idea of a cafeteria. After an initial trip, children would have been able to ask questions about what they wanted to observe or find out.

Teachers regularly ask children to pose questions before doing fieldwork. Children's questions about what they want to find out at the site, and how they will do so, are written on a chart. When the trip is taken, the chart is cut apart and each child, or group of children, is given a question strip to remind them of the questions they want answered.

Teachers give children clipboards and paper so children can document and record answers to their questions. One teacher divided the paper into four parts. In each part she drew a symbol to remind children of the purpose of the trip. On a visit to a plant nursery the symbols were a flower, a pot, a garden tool, and pile of dirt. These represented the questions children had prepared before the trip: "What kind of plants will we see? Where do the plants grow? What tools does the gardener use? What do plants need to grow?" Children documented their findings to these questions in the appropriate boxes.

Bringing along a science kit or two is helpful. After all, if children are to investigate, they need tools to measure, weigh, compare, and contrast and magnifying glasses so they can take a closer look. While visiting a fire station, children were enthralled with the size of the wheels of the trucks. Using a piece of yarn from the science kit, the length and width of the wheels were measured and the number of times the piece of yarn was used, recorded. Back in the classroom children used the yarn to find out how tall the filing cabinets, piano, and their desks were as compared to how tall the tires on the fire truck were.

To document children's learning, take digital photos of children asking questions, measuring, weighing, or observing. Not only do the photos document children's learning, but they help children recall their experiences and reflect on them when back in the classroom (see Figure 6.3).

At the end of the project additional questions are necessary: "What did we learn? What do we need to learn? What else would you like to know about . . . ?" Children can consult the photos taken while on the field trip, their clipboards, or their sketches of the things that interested them at the site to ask additional questions. Or children can continue to conduct further research by consulting experts, Web sites, factual books, videos, or CD clips.

Figure 6.3. Documenting Field Work

An inexpensive digital camera, or any other camera, enables the teacher to record children's experiences during fieldwork. A digital camera allows children to see immediate results. Later photos can be a source of information for children as they are asked to reach conclusions about their work, reflect on their experiences, or communicate their conclusions to others. Since prints can be readily made, a digital camera leads to publishing children's work to share with peers, the center or school, families, grandparents, and the larger community.

Analyzing

What do children's investigations mean? What did they find out? How do they explain what they found? The science standards maintain that children, even the youngest, can begin the process of learning what constitutes evidence. After an investigation, children are asked to give explanations for their findings. Their explanations should be based on the knowledge they have at hand. Children can support their explanations through further observations and questioning, or by checking their explanations with the experience and observations of others (NCR/NAS, 1996).

Teachers foster children's ability to analyze their findings and seek explanations by enabling them to classify their findings, compare and contrast their findings, order findings, and when appropriate compare their findings and ideas to those of others (Harlan & Rivkin, 2004).

Classifying. Young children naturally and spontaneously try to make sense of their world by classifying things in their world. Three-year-old Madeline collected a series of small bags with handles: Two were bags that had once contained her birthday gifts and two were purses, one hers, the other her mother's. Lining up the bags, Madeline makes collections. She puts plastic animals in one bag, pegs in another, and other things in the other two. Then dumping the bags out, she begins again, making different collections.

At home children have many opportunities to observe and classify things in their environment. The forks are together, separate from the spoons. Their socks are in one drawer, their T-shirts in another. Vegetables, breads, and fruits are a part of a meal, but dessert comes after the meal.

In school, teachers provide additional, more formal opportunities for classification. Centers of interests,

with like materials grouped together around a theme, are an example of intentional classification. Children learn that in the housekeeping area they'll find materials for dramatic play, in the block area materials to build with, and in the manipulative area things to count, sort, put together, or take apart.

Teachers provide materials for children to classify. Teachers might provide boxes of scrap materials; old greeting cards; a button box (with buttons too large to be stuffed anywhere); lotto games, dominoes, and board games; plastic farm, zoo, and wild animals; toy trucks and cars; plastic people; or natural objects such as rocks, shells, leaves, or acorns to sort and classify.

Giving children some type of sorting tray helps them classify. Egg cartons or any box that has dividers are helpful. Plastic glasses glued to a heavy piece of cardboard and a flannel board with yarn divisions are other useful sorting trays. It isn't necessary for children to use these trays, but having them present suggests sorting to children.

Comparing and contrasting. Children seem to compare and contrast naturally as they explore their world. When comparing, children establish a relationship between two objects on the basis of a specific attribute. Often their comparisons revolve around concepts of big and little: "This is the biggest." Teachers can guide children to make comparisons on the basis of other attributes, such as texture, shape, size, form, color, or taste.

Children can use blocks, sand and water, or art activities to develop the language of comparison and the ability to make comparisons. A box of material scraps leads children to compare materials that are soft and those that are rough. Blocks are compared by size and shape, those that are longer or shorter, and those that are squares or arches. Sand is compared and contrasted before and after water has been added, and the size and shape of the containers and tools for working with sand are compared and contrasted.

Children also make comparisons in terms of numbers. They should be encouraged to observe and question which is the longest or shortest, which things move slow or fast, or which group has more or less than another.

Ordering. Ordering, a prenumber skill, is another tool for analyzing information. Children probably come to school with some experience with ordering. They may have played with nesting blocks, rings in graduated sizes, or building towers, all based on the principle of ordering from smallest to largest.

In school, children will have additional experiences arranging objects in order. They may sort building toys

One class compared temperatures during February.

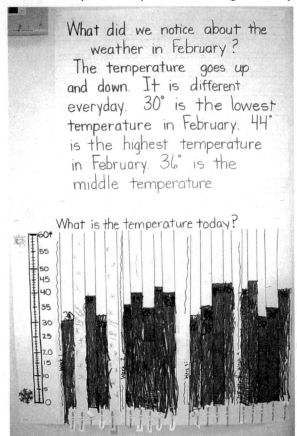

What did we notice about the weather in February?
The temperature goes up and down. It is different everyday. 30° is the lowest temperature in February. 44° is the highest temperature in February. 36° is the middle temperature.

What is the temperature today?

and parquet blocks in order from shortest to longest. Or they may weigh objects using a balance scale to find out which of the objects is the heaviest and which is the lightest.

Comparing ideas with those of others. An argument persisted about whether or not worms could see. After the children made astute and careful observations of worms in different situations, the teacher put a few books about worms on the library table. Children consulted these, looked at the pictures, and then looked at the worms again. The teacher read some of the facts about worms to the children. Using the authors as experts, the children finally reached the conclusion that worms didn't have eyes, but they could still find their way around because they sensed—"somehow, it may be magic," was one child's explanation—where to move.

Reaching Conclusions and Communicating Results to Others

"What did you find?" "What do you think?" asks the teacher. And children, as scientists, answer. "I found out that worms don't have legs; they move their muscles and crawl all around."

Scientists reach conclusions, and when they do so, they are obligated to communicate their conclusions to others. Scientists may write books and scientific papers or present their findings and conclusions at conferences or other meetings of learned societies. Once an idea has been communicated, discussion and even argument takes place. When scientists present their conclusions to others, they must be prepared to defend their ideas and to articulate why they believe these ideas. Considering other points of view leads to constructing additional investigations. It's in this process that new ideas, new ways of thinking, are formulated (Henderson, 2001).

Children will not present their ideas about worms in a learned journal or present them at a conference. They can, however, learn to organize their ideas in order to communicate these to others, and children can present their ideas to their group and to others outside of the group. Children need the opportunities to think, reflect, and organize their ideas. Taking the time and building the opportunities for children to reflect and think is not a fad or an add-on to the curriculum, but rather the core concept of education (Halpern, 2004).

Group meetings. Instead of a show-and-tell during morning meeting when plans for the day and news were shared and discussed, one teacher held a group meeting after work time. At this group meeting children were invited to tell about what they had accomplished during work time. Children showed their paintings or constructions, or asked the group to gather and look at their block buildings. Others told of how they tried to join materials together and what they did and did not accomplish. Ideas on how to do so were shared.

The meeting provided a forum for children to discuss their conclusions from their inquiries as well. For example, the group studying worms presented what they had found out about worms to the rest of the children, with illustrations and books to back up their ideas.

Group meetings are also opportunities for children to dictate their ideas of their scientific discoveries and experiences. Dictating as a group builds a sense of community. All children can participate and make contributions at their own level. (See Figure 6.4 for an example of a group dictation.)

Drawing, painting, building. Art is another language for learning. Children express their ideas, emotions, and experiences through drawing, painting, constructing, and writing. Provide children with art materials that enable them to reflect on their experiences. A group of children took a trip to the city where they marveled at the tall buildings. Back in the classroom, the teacher featured block building by enlarging the block building area and adding books on building skyscrapers to the area. Long strips of brown paper

Figure 6.4. Recording Children's Experiences

The Plant Store

We went to a plant store.
They sell plants and flowers and trees.
A plant store is called a plant nursery.
We like the plant store.

[*Experience story dictated following a trip to a nursery*]

were added to the painting and drawing areas. Children used these to draw and paint the tall buildings they saw.

After a trip to see cherry trees in bloom, another teacher placed white and red paints at the easels. Children mixed the two colors together to make pink. "Look, look," said one child after mixing red and white together, "I discovered pink." This discovery was later demonstrated during group meeting. Blank books, made of a couple of pieces of paper stapled together, can be available in the writing area for children to write about their discoveries.

See Figure 6.5 for how to share children's work with families and the community on a web site.

USING SCIENTIFIC-INQUIRY SKILLS TO FULFILL SCIENCE CONTENT STANDARDS

This section illustrates how the skills of science inquiry form the foundation for children's study of content from the physical and life sciences and technology. For each of the science content areas, a list of standards is given, followed by several descriptions of extended projects for that area. These descriptions tell how children investigated content identified in specific standards, identify vocabulary words introduced, and end with a statement of the science standards experienced by the children.

Figure 6.5. Make the Home-School Connection (Science)

Teachers have found class or school web sites useful in communicating not only what the children do but the results of their inquiries as well. When teachers scan children's artwork, photos of their experiences, charts, and other information, and post the documentation on a web site, families and the school community will be able to have access to children's scientific inquiries.

The Physical Sciences

Standards for the physical sciences call for children to

- Observe the properties of materials, including size, weight, shape, color, temperature, and the ability to react with other substances
- Investigate these properties through measuring using tools, such as rulers, balances, and thermometers
- Become familiar with the concept that materials can exist in several states
- Describe objects by the properties of the materials from which they are made

Exploring balls. Collect a number of different sizes and types of balls, such as softballs, plastic beach balls, rubber balls, hard plastic balls for rolling, or small rubber balls attached to boards with strings.

Let children play around with the balls, finding out what they can do with each of them. Keep the exploration of balls informal and spontaneous. Teachers of very young children might have them sit on the floor with legs spread apart, and roll large balls to different children who can catch them with their hands and legs. Four- and five-year-olds learn to catch a ball when it's bounced just once, close to them. Sometimes the teacher will work with one or two children who are interested in the balls, other times with just one child. There may also be times when the teacher asks the entire group to gather and poses a problem for them to solve sometime during their work time.

Ask individual children playing with balls, "What are balls made of?" Have them use magnifying glasses to explore the surfaces of the balls. Talk about the texture—how each ball feels. Compare and contrast the balls in terms of size, weight, color, and usefulness. Have pieces of yarn or string ready for children to measure the circumference of the balls. Provide large boxes for children to categorize the balls by material, size, color, or any other attribute they choose. Give children time to explore.

On another day find out what balls can do. Call the group together and ask them to find out how the balls behave. Show them how to drop a ball from a prespecified height onto a surface. Ask children to observe what happens when they drop different balls from the same height onto the same surface. Older children might try to measure how high each different ball bounces on the surface. Now change the surface. Instead of the floor, add a cushion of foam rubber and ask the children to try their experiment again. What happens to the balls when dropped from the same height onto the foam? Observe children and listen for their questions. Do they ask why? Advance explanations? Follow up on their questions and explanations.

What can balls do?

Document children's work through graphs or charts showing which balls bounce the highest or lowest on different surfaces. Depending on children's interest, the teacher may chart the different uses balls have. Some are for playing ball, others, for bouncing or for swimming. Document children's explorations through digital photographs so children can reflect on their experiences.

Throughout the exploration of balls, which could continue as long as children are interested, use the vocabulary of science:

Soft or hard
High or low
Smooth or rough
Large or small
Fast or slow

Conclude the study of balls by asking children what they've learned about balls. Record their comments on experience charts or make a book using children's comments and the photos taken of them working with balls. Through this project, the children experienced the physical science standards that *objects are made of differing materials, these materials can be named and described,* and *properties of materials can be observed, named, and measured.*

Planes, trains, and automobiles. Use the trucks, cars, trains, or other vehicles children bring to school with them, or provide a collection of wheeled toys. The point of this investigation is to have children observe the different materials the toys are made of and investigate what wheeled toys can do.

Freely and spontaneously, children can group, categorize, compare, and contrast the vehicles. Provide a tablecloth marked off into sections so they can categorize the vehicles by type, color, size, or whatever attribute

they wish. Older children might group the vehicles by where they travel—in the air, on water, or on land.

Talk about the materials the cars are made of and how they are made. Ask children to examine the cars and vehicles and name the things they are made of. Children might find their cars are made of

Rubber	Cloth
Metal	Wood
Plastic	Nuts and bolts
Vinyl	Screws

Experiment a bit. Ask children to build a ramp using a piece of wood propped up with a block. Ask them to roll different vehicles down the ramp and measure how fast and far each goes. Put a mark on the floor to measure how far each vehicle goes. Have children experiment with raising and lowering the ramp using other blocks and observing the results.

Brainstorm with the children about who made the cars and trucks. The point is to introduce the idea that some materials are made by humans. Then ask children for their ideas of a perfect car. What would they include in their perfect car? List their ideas on a chart. Now offer children an assortment of junk. Boxes, paper tubes, pieces of cloth, pie pans, old wheels from discarded toys, yarn and string, tape and joining materials, scissors, and paper. The directions are "Create a car, plane, truck, or train that you will drive when you are a teenager." (See Figure 6.6 for suggestions for including children with special needs in this project.)

Document children's discoveries. Hold a group meeting to dictate a newsletter to be sent to families describing children's experiences with planes, trains, and automobiles. Ask children to tell about their discoveries or their inventions. Through this project, the

Figure 6.6. Including Children with Special Needs in Scientific Inquiry

---

Children with special needs can be included in exploring planes, trains, and automobiles if adaptations are made.

• Arrange for wheelchair-accessible tables so children do not have to be on the floor to experiment with the cars and ramps.

• Plan times for children with a hearing impairment to work with the materials one-on-one with another child or in small groups so they can focus on hearing the other children.

---

children experienced the physical science standards that *objects are made of differing materials* and *properties of materials, including their speed, can be measured.*

Dissolving things. *Dissolve* means to break up a connection or to make a solution. Dissolving things gives children experience with the idea that materials can exist in several states. The vocabulary you will use includes the following words:

Dissolve
Solution
Sweet or sour
Liquid or solid

Begin with the familiar. If it is a hot day, make lemonade, or if it is a cold day, make cocoa using a powdered mix. After children have squeezed a number of lemons and diluted the juice with water, start the process of adding sugar to the lemonade. Start with just a teaspoon of sugar in the pitcher. Stir until the sugar is dissolved. Ask children where the sugar went. Try dissolving a teaspoon of sugar in some lemonade in a small dish. Watch what happens. Taste the lemonade; is it sweet or sour? Add another teaspoon of sugar. Now have children predict what will happen to the sugar. Repeat until the lemonade is sweet enough for drinking.

If it is a cold day, make one-cup cocoa. You'll need an aide or volunteer to supervise as all the children will make their own cup of cocoa. Provide a pitcher of heated milk that children can handle themselves with supervision. Have children measure a tablespoonful of cocoa powder into a cup. Ask children what they think will happen when the heated milk is added. See if their predictions take place.

On another day set up a discovery table. On the table place clear plastic cups and small wooden sticks for stirring. Place a child-manageable pitcher of water that can be refilled as needed. Fill other clear plastic containers with sand, rocks, marbles, baby powder, sugar, salt, coffee grounds, and other materials. Have children experiment and find out what will or will not dissolve. Use clipboards marked with two columns, one headed by the word *yes*, the other *no*. Children are to experiment with different materials and sketch the material under the correct column, either yes the material dissolved, or no it did not.

Discuss the experiment during meeting time. What did children discover? Record children's experiences with dissolving at the discovery table through digital photos. Record their comments while working at the table, and when talking as a group about dissolving (see Figure 6.7). Ask children to draw what they saw happening when they made cocoa, lemonade, or worked at the discovery table. Through their investigations, the

Figure 6.7. Documenting Children's Experiences

What Dissolves?

We put stuff in water.
Some things turn into the water.
You cannot see them again.
Some things do not dissolve.
Dissolve is a new word.

[*Experience chart dictated after experimenting with dissolving*]

children experienced the physical science standard that *materials can exist in several states.*

The Life Sciences

Standards from the life sciences call for children to understand the following things:

- Living organisms have basic needs.
- Each plant or animal has different structures that serve different functions in growth, survival, and reproduction.
- The behavior of individual organisms is influenced by interior and external cues.
- Plants and animals have life cycles.
- Characteristics of an organism are inherited from the parents of the organism.

Studying mealworms. Obtain mealworms from a pet store or worm supply store such as Rainbow Mealworms (2,000 mealworms cost about $10). A terrarium is also needed to raise the mealworms in. Teachers of primary-aged children could have each child construct individual mealworm containers using any clear plastic box or container. The containers or terrarium can be filled with oat bran, and every 2 weeks a slice of apple, potato, or lettuce leaves can be provided for food. Mealworms in the larva stage will molt, then go into a white pupa stage, and then turn into adult beetles.

The mealworms will arrive in newspaper in the larva stage. Shake them from the newspaper into the terrarium. Ask children what they see. Take out a few worms and ask children to speculate on what the name of the worms is. Put some mealworms on a piece of paper for individual children or teams of children to observe. Ask children to look at the mealworms. What word would they use to describe its shape? Have the children look again, from a different direction.

Take the time to listen and respond to children's questions. "Wait, wait," said one 4-year-old, as a teacher went on with ideas for observing the mealworms. "I asked a lot of questions, and you didn't answer even one." The teacher slowed down, brought chart paper and a marker to the table of mealworms, and said, "Let's begin again. What questions do you have?" She recorded the children's questions: "What are the names of these worms?" "What do they do?" "What do they eat?" "Why are they in my room? I don't like them." "Do they have legs?" "How do they see?" As she recorded the questions, the teacher responded to some, naming the worms. To the others she asked the children how they might find the answers.

Each day the group picked a question to answer. They used magnifying glasses to see if the mealworm is divided into parts. They used the glasses to look for other body parts, such as eyes or legs. The children squatted down so they could see the mealworms on their table at eye level and could observe in what direction the mealworms moved. Different foods were placed in the terrarium and children recorded which foods seemed to please the mealworms the best. The children thought the mealworms ate more of the apple slice than they did of the piece of lettuce.

After children observed the worms for several days, the group met again. The teacher recorded the answers to some of the questions on the chart. The teacher used the children's questions and answers to make a book entitled "What We Learned About Mealworms." The children drew their perceptions of the mealworms to illustrate the book.

At some point older children could compare and contrast mealworms with red worms they find on the play yard or sidewalk after the rain. How are they alike and how are they different?

When mealworms begin to turn into pupas, ask children to speculate on what is happening and record this in pictures or writing. List their questions and ideas. Keep a blank calendar next to the mealworm container so children can mark off the number of days the pupa stage takes. After the beetle stage has been completed, children can be asked to tell what they learned about mealworms, including what they need to live and the stages of their life cycle. This would be a good time to consult books about the life cycle of mealworms or bring in an expert, perhaps an older child in elementary school who has studied mealworms, to talk with the children.

During this project the vocabulary children can learn include the following words:

Mealworm
Oat bran
Larva
Pupa
Beetle

Studying mealworms provided an opportunity for children to experience the life science standards that *living organisms have basic needs; each plant or animal has different structures that serve different functions in growth, survival, and reproduction;* and *plants and animals have life cycles.*

Blooming things. A study of blossoms will take a number of weeks, and teachers will need to look at a lot of different plants, trees, or shrubs that are in bud and blossom. The goal is to study the wide variety of plant life around the children. Before starting the study, ask children to draw a picture of a flower, or a blossom if they know the word *blossom*. Save these in children's portfolios.

As the plants around the school begin to blossom, ask the children to focus their observations on the buds and blossoms. Take a walk around the school to find plants that are blooming. Give children clipboards so they can count and sketch the blooming plants they find. Take along a couple of viewing tubes and a few science kits.

In another activity the teacher might place a circle of yarn around a spot on the sidewalk or play yard and name all the plants that are inside the circle. Have the children use the viewing tubes to find the three most common blooming plants on the play yard or in the cracks of the sidewalk. Name these for children. Focus children's observations on where plants are growing. How do plants grow in the cracks of the sidewalk? What plants grow in the shade? Which are growing in full sun?

Give the children the magnifying glasses from the science kits to observe the blossoms on different plants.

Living organisms have basic needs.

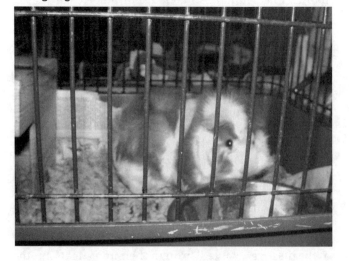

What do children see? Ask children to name the shapes of the petals they see. What colors are the blossoms?

Guide the children to compare and contrast blossoms on different plants, or even on the same plant. The blossoms of an elm tree will differ from those on a maple tree, which will, in turn, differ from blossoms on fruit trees (Humphreys, 2000). Make charts of blossoms that have petals and those that do not.

Have the children measure the blossoms. Which blossom is the largest? The smallest? Or are they all about the same size? One group decided to find the longest and shortest petals on the flowers around them. They found a tiny, tiny flower, barely visible without a magnifying glass, on weeds growing low to the ground. "It's so tiny you can't measure it," the children concluded. And they found a sunflower growing under the bird feeder and declared its petals the longest ever.

On another day help the children examine where the blossoms grow on trees or shrubs. They may find some that are symmetrical, growing directly opposite each other on a branch, or they may find blossoms that alternate on a branch. Others may grow haphazardly, or paired. Encourage children to feel the texture of the blossoms. Some may be smooth and translucent, others furry and tough. Which of the blossoms have veins?

Continue the study by taking walks to observe blossoms losing their petals and the fruit or seedpods developing. Ask children to predict what will happen. What kind of fruit do they think will grow on a cherry tree? What will the seeds of the maple tree look like?

It is important for children to reach conclusions about their investigations. They need a way to reflect on their season of studying blossoms. They can draw, paint, or construct blossoms of collage materials (see Figure 6.8) and document their ideas by creating books describing their observations of how blossoms bud, grow, and develop into fruit or seeds. The vocabulary children learned during the study include the following words:

Petal
Stamen
Pistil
Vein
Rough or smooth
Symmetrical or alternating

By studying blossoms, the children experienced the life science standards that *each plant or animal has different structures that serve different functions in growth, survival, and reproduction* and *plants and animals have life cycles.* For another example of children studying the life sciences, see the "Sample Investigation" at the end of the chapter.

Figure 6.8. Assessing Drawings from a Scientific View

Compare the drawings children make of blossoms at the beginning of the study to those they complete at the end of the study. Observe and record for both beginning and final drawings:

- Number of details
- Completeness
- Number of different colors used
- Number of materials used
- Increase in realism

Technology

The technology standards ask children to become aware of the following things:

- Some objects occur in nature; others have been designed and made by people to solve human problems.
- People create, invent, and design tools and techniques to solve problems.
- Tools help scientists make better observations, measurements, and equipment for investigations.

Clothes we wear. Look at children's clothing in a new way. The technologies used to fasten children's clothing—buttons, zippers, Velcro, shoestrings, buckles—were each the invention of a person. Begin by asking children to examine how their clothing is fastened.

One teacher began with a study of shoes. Three- and four-year-old children had visited a shoe store and then set up a shoe store in their class. Using the foot measures the store lent them, children measured each other's feet and shoes with glee. Taking children's interest in shoes one step further, the teacher asked children the question, "How do your shoes stay on?" Children said they "just did." Others said, "Mine have Velcro" or "I have shoestrings." The number of children who wore shoes without any fastener and those whose shoes had strings, buckles, or Velcro were counted and graphed.

Children's interest in fasteners expanded and a study of the way children's coats were fastened took place. Zippers were examined, different sizes and shapes of buttons were counted and graphed, and different buckles and ties were counted and compared. Hats and how they were made to stay on one's head were other objects of study.

During the project, the vocabulary children learned included the following words:

Fasteners
Inventor
Created
Velcro
Buckle

To close the study of fasteners, the children were asked to create a new way of keeping shoes on their feet. Boxes of old ties, material, large paper clips, staplers, glue, papers, fasteners, and markers were provided to permit children full exploration of their imaginations. The shoes that resulted were wild and funny, and the group all agreed that strings, Velcro, and buckles were more practical than their creations. The idea, however, was that children were acting just like the inventors who at one time designed a new way of keeping shoes on feet.

Through this project, the children were able to experience the technology standards that *some objects occur in nature and others have been designed and made by people to solve human problems* and *people create, invent, and design tools and techniques to solve problems.*

Computers. From preschool through the early primary grades, children can explore and use computers.

People create and invent tools. One child constructed her own computer.

Three- and four-year-olds will play with computers, exploring and finding out what they can do and how. Teachers are available to offer a suggestion or guide children to achieve a goal, but the focus is on children's exploration. The goal is for children to solve their own problems and, at the same time, gain the basic skills of using the mouse and keyboard. Once skills are developed, children can use the computer to find information and to create and communicate with others as in the following example.

One kindergarten studied pets. The children graphed the pets they had. They visited a veterinarian's office and found out more about how to care for pets. The children's interests in animals other than their own pets began when the teacher asked them to think about and draw animals they knew could never be pets. Children drew and painted lions and tigers, elephants and antelopes, giant turtles and monkeys, as well as totally imaginary pets.

Using the computer, children searched for information on the animals they knew could never be their pets. Without going to the zoo or wildlife preserve, the children watched film clips of snow leopards, tigers, lions, elephants and great white sharks.

The vocabulary children learned included the following words:

Mouse
Keyboard
Computer program
Wild animals
Zoo animals
Veterinarian
Snow leopard

When their study was completed, children used the computer to put together a booklet of "Animals—Pets and Not Pets." They used the computer to write, or dictate, stories about their pet, and the animals they knew could never be pets. Using a drawing program, children illustrated their ideas. The booklet was printed and shared with the children's families, other kindergarten classrooms, and school administrators. Through this project, the children were able to experience the technology standards that *tools help scientists make better observations, measurements, and equipment for investigations.*

IN SUMMARY

- By engaging in scientific inquiry, children gain the process skills as well as learn content from the standards for the physical and life sciences and technology.
- Scientific inquiry involves learning to observe, question, investigate, analyze, and reach conclusions.

- Implementing the process of scientific inquiry leads to an integrated curriculum.

SAMPLE INVESTIGATION: CHILDREN STUDY THEIR PLAY YARD

Scientific Inquiry—Life Sciences

What better place to study the variety of living things than out of doors? The play yard offers children opportunities to observe what lives on their earth and how.

Selected standards

Observe objects and living things.
Investigate life processes.
Develop and record conclusions.

Activities

Toddlers (two–three years old)

- Name living things as children notice them. Give children the names of birds they see—pigeons, crows,

The play yard offers children opportunities to observe what lives on their earth and how.

robins, and so on. Name the trees that may be on the play yard and any plants or animals.
- Provide toddlers with a variety of empty cardboard boxes to push, move around, or sit in on the play yard. Depending on the resources on your play yard, toddlers can use boxes to collect fall leaves, acorns, pinecones, or rocks and stones. With the boxes and something to put in them, toddlers love to fill and spill over and over again. As they do so, name the items they are filling the boxes with and spilling out.

Preschoolers (three–four years old)

Ask children to make observations of living things in the play yard.

- What lives in and on the earth? To find out, take a piece of yarn and loop it in a circle on the grass or other play area suitable for digging. Have children use small shovels to dig the earth in this circle, and sift it through a framed screen into a bucket. Without disturbing the living things the children find, name and identify any insects, worms, grubs, acorns, or seeds that are beginning to sprout. Carefully replace the living things back in the earth. Have children use clipboards and markers to sketch their findings and write about what they found.
- Are there any rocks or equipment placed directly on the ground? If so, turn these over and see what life is found. The teacher should do this first without the children present in case there are scorpions or other things that might be harmful to children. If safe, ask children to predict what they might find living under a rock or piece of equipment. Then turn over the rock, and examine the life they find. Bring clipboards so children can draw their findings.

Kindergarten children (four–five years old)

- Prepare a place on the play yard for seed planting. Turn the earth over to make a planting bed.
- Meet with the children as a group. Show children packets of a variety of seeds (flower, bean, peas, and so on). Ask children to select a partner or pair children together. Each team will select a packet of seeds. Outside, the teams take turns planting the seeds.
- Back inside the classroom have each team report on what kind of seed they planted and what they expect to grow. Place the empty seed pack on a chart. Over time record when each type of seed sprouted, their growth, and the type of flower, bud, and fruit or vegetable each produced. Teams take turns making sure the seeds are watered and cared for. Talk about what seeds and plants need to grow. The point is

to acquaint children with the variety of plant life and the conditions seeds need to sprout, grow, and produce.

- Document children's learning by having them observe and draw or paint the seed, sprout, and full grown plant.

Assessing Children's Learning

Observe

- Note questions children ask. Pay attention to movement from rhetorical questions to those asked for a purpose.

- Notice children's observation strategies. Record length of attending; involvement; number of methods used; when, where, and what children observe.

Interview

- Ask individual children to tell you all they know about specific animal and/or plant life on the play yard. Record children's responses. Repeat the question periodically during the year, and note changes in children's ideas about living things.
- Ask individual children to reach conclusions about living and nonliving things on the play yard. Record their responses.

CHAPTER 7

Integrating the Arts Standards

When people discuss educational standards, they are generally talking about standards of learning for reading and mathematics. What children should achieve in reading and mathematics, when they should learn various skills, and how they should perform these skills, are the questions of the day. One rarely hears discussions about what children should be learning in the arts. With the focus on the privileged domains of reading and mathematics (NRC, 2001b), people too often fail to realize the importance of the arts in the curriculum. All of the arts—the visual arts, theatre, music, and dance—considered by many as "soft" domains, are as integral to children's cognitive and academic achievement as they are to the total curriculum.

Dance, Music, Theatre, Visual Arts: What Every Young American Should Know and Be Able to Do in the Arts (CNAEA, 1994) made clear that knowledge of and skills in the arts are just as critical to children's school success as are reading and mathematics. Experiences with the arts are foundational for the development of symbolic and abstract thought, which is prerequisite to learning to read. When children participate in the arts, nothing has been predetermined for them. They are forced to think, make choices, question, and reflect on their ideas. Recognizing the arts as integral to children's thinking and valid in and of themselves, the Goals 2000: Educate America Act of 1994 acknowledged that the arts are a core subject, as important to education as English, mathematics, or any other subject.

Standards for arts education ensure that the intent of Goals 2000 will be fulfilled and present a vision of effective arts education. The standards do not provide a mold for all children and their teachers to fit into, but rather they present the content, expectations for student experiences, and levels for student achievement.

The goals for this chapter are to

- Present the national standards for the arts—the visual arts, theatre, music, and dance

- Describe the integration of the arts as creative thinking into the total curriculum
- Illustrate the implementation of the standards for the visual arts, theatre, music, and dance

STANDARDS FOR THE VISUAL ARTS, THEATRE, MUSIC, AND DANCE

The arts standards that follow should be considered as examples of those that may be presented to teachers. I derived these from the arts standards published in 1994 by the Consortium of the National Arts Education Associations (CNAEA) and now available online at ArtsEdge (http://artsedge.kennedy-center.org/teach/standards/). The arts standards are both declarative and procedural in nature. They define the arts content children should know as well as what children should be able to do in the arts in kindergarten–Grade 4, Grades 5–8, Grades 9–12, and Grades 9–12 advanced.

As the arts standards begin with the kindergarten, those pertaining to older children were excluded from my list. The selection of standards for early childhood was guided by McREL's *Content Knowledge: A Compendium of Standards and Benchmarks* for K–12 Education (Kendall & Marzano, 2004) and the *Pre-K Standards* of CTB/McGraw-Hill (2002).

1. The visual arts. Children will:
   1.a. Explore and gain mastery over a variety of art media
   1.b. Select from different media, techniques, and processes in order to express and communicate their ideas, experiences, and feelings
   1.c. Use art media and tools responsibly
   1.d. Recognize and talk about line, texture, color, and space
   1.e. Recognize their own artwork and that of others

2. Theatre. Children will:
   2.a. Participate in sociodramatic playgroups
   2.b. Be able to take on a role when engaged in creative dramatics
3. Music. Children will:
   3.a. Learn to listen and identify musical sounds
   3.b. Use rhythm instruments to create music alone or with a group, and be able to echo short rhythmic patterns
   3.c. Use their voices to make music
4. Dance. Children will:
   4.a. Develop the ability to control and execute rhythmic movements
   4.b. Develop the ability to listen to music, execute rhythmic movements, and put the two together

INTEGRATING THE ARTS INTO THE CURRICULUM

Even without the pressure of school reform and accountability, reading and mathematics would probably dominate the school curriculum. The vast body of research documenting the power of language and mathematics learning during the early years cannot be ignored. Obviously, children must be able to read and compute. But to develop into successful, contributing members of a democratic society, they must also be able to think and create. This means schools must develop all of children's thinking and creative skills, not just so children can be successful in the complex world of the future, but so they can live lives rich in meaning today (CNAEA, 1994).

The arts—visual, dance, music, and theatre—are unique in that they are a platform for developing children's thinking and creative abilities (Coakley, 1997; Gardiner, Fox, Knowles, & Jeffrey, 1996). When creat-

Creating and problem solving go together.

ing in the visual, musical, or theatrical arts, children are the ones who are engaged in thinking skills, not the teacher. Children must think of an experience, feeling, or idea, and struggle internally to find symbols and ways to express these, and the tools and media to do so. Because of its symbolic nature, art is in fact a language (Seefeldt, 1995). In the process of producing art, children set goals, make plans to achieve these goals, and monitor their progress toward goal attainment. They are the ones who do the work, and they are the ones who experience the internal joy and satisfaction that comes from thinking and creating.

In doing so, children not only are using symbolic modes of thought and expression, but are developing the realization that others may have alternate or different ways of thinking and expressing their ideas, thoughts, and feelings. Looking at the artwork of others and discussing it, children begin to understand, respect, and appreciate views that may differ from their own.

Research demonstrates that children do learn thinking skills when participating in the arts (Winner & Hetland, 2000). Children who participated in music activities, for example, made higher IQ gains than children who did not take part in any music groups because, according to Schellenberg (2003), music education provided for periods of focused attention, memorization, and concentration.

Positive gains in language growth have frequently been related to the inclusion of the arts in the curriculum (Althouse, Johnson, & Mitchell, 2003); that is, when children have teachers who are knowledgeable about the arts and about how to discuss the arts with children and respond to their ideas, questions, and work (Douglas & Schwartz, 1967; Hogg & McWhinnie, 1968).

Then too, when the curriculum is united around the processes of problem solving, the arts are essential. Making art or music, or participating in creative dramatics or dance, children develop skills of observation and learn to examine the objects and events of their lives. At the same time, they grow in their ability to describe, interpret, and evaluate (CNAEA, 1994).

In Reggio Emilia, a town in northern Italy noted for its outstanding early care and education, problem solving is at the core of the curriculum. The arts are not a separate part of the curriculum, but are thought of as just one more way for children to experience problem solving (Althouse et al., 2003).

THE VISUAL ARTS

Although the arts are integral to the total curriculum, this integration does not deny a specific focus on teaching visual arts. It is the very nature of the visual arts, however, that connects them to nearly every curriculum

Figure 7.1. The Visual Arts Are Integral to the Entire Curriculum

Thinking

Throughout the process of making art, children are involved in questioning, solving problems, analyzing their ideas, and reaching conclusions. Because art is another language for learning, the products that result from children's work serve to communicate ideas, feelings, and experiences to others.

Language Learning

Creating in the visual arts increases children's vocabularies. Children learn the names of differing media and the tools they use. Verbs are learned as children give names to their actions, and adjectives and adverbs are used to describe their work and that of others. Creating art is another way of knowing and communicating.

Science

Creating visual arts demands observing. Working with different media introduces children to the nature and characteristics of a variety of physical materials and to the ideas of how, why, and when matter changes.

Mathematics

As they paint, cut, and paste, children will be asked to measure, weigh, and consider length, volume, width, and shape. Patterns are observed and created.

Physical Development

Development of small-muscle skills, especially those involved in learning to write, stem from work in the visual arts, which demand children coordinate their thoughts with their hands and learn to control tools.

content area (see Figure 7.1). Children "learn *through* art in the context of their learning in other areas of the classroom curriculum" (Althouse et al., 2003, pp. 2–3).

The visual arts are comprised of a number of disciplines. These range from drawing, painting, sculpture, and design, to architecture, film, video, and folk arts (CNAEA, 1994). A wide range of materials and tools are involved in working with the visual arts. Children have the opportunity to communicate their ideas and feelings, leaving their mark with crayons, markers, paints, modeling, and construction materials or other media.

Because the visual arts are so connected to everything else that takes place in good schools for young children, the task of fulfilling the arts standards is readily achievable. First, children need to have something to think about—some idea, feeling, emotion, or experience to express. Then they need art materials, and the space and time to use them. Finally, children need to learn the language of art and the skills involved in talking about the visual arts.

Experiences

If children are to fulfill the arts standard of *selecting from different media, techniques, and processes in order to express and communicate their ideas, experiences, and feelings*, they first must have something to think about or feel. Firsthand, meaningful experiences provided through a curriculum organized around projects, themes, or units gives children the ideas, feelings, and thoughts that push for expression (see Figure 7.2). The visual arts give children the opportunity not only to express these ideas and feelings, but to reflect on their experiences. Expressing their thoughts through drawing, painting, modeling, and constructing gives children a way to think about their own ideas and to refine, rethink, and clarify them.

Although implementing a project or thematic approach to children's learning means children will have numerous meaningful learning experiences (see "Sample Investigation" at the end of the chapter), not all experiences need stem from the project approach. The materials of the visual arts themselves give children something to think about and express. Experiencing paints running together, feeling clay squish between their fingers, feeling the smoothness of wood and experiencing its hardness, motivates children to expression. Handling and feeling different types of paper, folding paper, tearing it, motivates children to using paper to express their ideas.

Figure 7.2. Characteristics of Meaningful Experiences

- *Real.* They stem from children's firsthand experiences with their here-and-now world.

- *Of deep personal interest.* Children, like all humans, learn best when they are personally involved and interested in their learning.

- *Significant in terms of content.* They are based on concepts or ideas key to a given discipline.

- *Continuous.* One experience leads to another, forming a unified whole.

The arts stem from children's personal experiences. Harper drew a picture of his birthday cake.

Even vicarious experiences—while not as strong as firsthand experiences—give children something to think about and express. For example, children may write and illustrate their own version of the *Snowy Day* (Keats, 1963), paint where the "wild things" live when not in Max's bedroom, or create a map of where the gingerbread boy ran. The point is that when the curriculum is meaningful to children, and based on children's explorations of their world, children have much to reflect on and express through art. There is no need for teachers to find something new to do every day because children's ideas and the need to express them are full, rich, and new each day.

Materials

To achieve the standards of *exploring and gaining mastery over a variety of art media, selecting media, techniques, and processes to express and communicate ideas*, and *using art media and tools responsibly*, children must be provided with a wide variety of materials:

- Drawing materials—markers, crayons, pencils, chalk, and pastels
- Papers of different weights and textures, as well as plenty of newsprint for scribblers
- Scissors and cutting tools
- Pastes, glues, and tapes
- Staplers and joiners
- Paints—fluid, cake, and powdered tempera and also water colors
- Fabric scraps, scrap upholstery material
- Building materials—boxes, tubes
- Trims—yarns, strings, ribbons
- Collage materials, especially as natural materials

- Modeling materials—clay, dough, quick-dry claylike materials

How the materials are arranged and offered to children makes a difference in how the standards will be implemented. Arranging materials on low shelves in open boxes so children can see choices fulfills the standard of selecting materials to express their ideas. Pre-categorizing the materials, with all of one type of media presented together, helps children become knowledgeable of the materials that are available.

Young children do not have to have vast amounts or many different types of media. Their needs are simple. Each day children should have something with which to draw, paint, model, construct, cut, and paste. When working with 3- or 4-year-olds, teachers have found it useful to provide just one kind of material for each media choice at a time; for example, chunky crayons and newsprint may be the materials for drawing, and clay for modeling. Giving children time to find out what they can do with a specific material—for example, how the crayon acts when pressed or how to use the crayon to fill in spaces—gives children the opportunity to explore.

Children learn to master media.

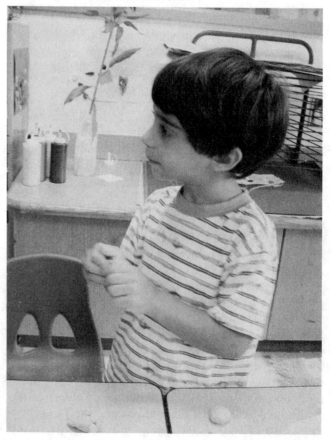

When children are exploring paints, it's not necessary to have every color available. Children first must feel mastery over the material before being able to select from a variety of colors, or different types of paint, in order to give expression to their ideas. Once children develop skill with this medium and really come to know its uses, then other materials can be added. Gradually, they will gain mastery over a variety of art materials.

Letting children linger with the same medium and tools helps them learn how to select materials appropriate to their needs. When children understand a medium, then they are able to select specific materials to use in ways that can fully express their ideas, reflect their experiences, and release emotions.

Talking About Art

If children are to be able to *recognize and talk about line, texture, color, and space* and *recognize their own art work and that of others*, their teachers must be skilled at talking about art. Teachers model talking about art, explicitly teaching children the concepts and language of art. When talking with children about their artwork, or the artwork of others, teachers can discuss the content of the work and describe line, color (hue, value, intensity), shape, space, form, texture, and composition (see Figure 7.3 for definitions of these art terms).

Talking to children about their art is a skill. There are few guidelines, however, about when and how to talk to children about their art. No one wants to interrupt a child struggling to draw ears on a rabbit with a discussion about line or shape. And watching children totally engaged in splashing paint on paper, one somehow knows that talking about color at this time would not be appropriate.

Yet, talking with children about art will be necessary to introduce children to concepts of art, as well as achieve the standards. Sensitive teachers are able to comment on children's work, or engage children in conversation about their work, without interrupting children's thought processes. It seems productive to describe what children are doing: "You're moving your crayon all across the paper." "You're thinking about what you are doing." "You mixed red and white and made a new shade of pink."

At times, a suggestion or two will help children find a solution to a problem, such as "Hold the scissors like this" or "What else could you use?" (Althouse et al., 2003). Seriously talking with children about what they are trying to do is rewarding: "Where did you get this idea?" "How were you able to join these two pieces?" Scaffolding, by following children's lead, responding to what they already know, and building on this help children gain concepts of art.

Figure 7.3. Using the Vocabulary of Art

Line

A basic structural element of art. Line describes the contour of a three-dimensional object. Lines are considered a continuous mark on a surface.

Talk about lines in children's artwork, describing lines as *sweeping, vertical, horizontal, strong, curved, wide, narrow, zigzag, diagonal, bending, fast, straight, blurred, smooth, lumpy, crooked, broken, up and down, slow, thin, rough,* or *overlapping.*

Color

A visual sensation of light. The three characteristics of color are hue, value, and intensity. *Hue* is the color name, *value* is the color's quality, meaning the amount of light or dark it contains, and *intensity* refers to the brightness or dullness of a color. Adding complementary colors, such as green to red, deepens or dulls the base color.

Talk about color in children's work, describing color by naming the colors used, and talking about the color's *brightness, lightness,* or *darkness.*

Shape and Form

The contours of an object, or enclosed space.

Talk about shape in children's work, describing shapes by naming shapes as *circle, square, rectangle, triangle, oval, diamond, free-form,* and talking about their size (e.g., *large* or *small*) and texture (*smooth* or *rough*).

Texture

The surface quality of an artwork.

Talk about texture in children's work, describing their marks as: *smooth, rough, natural, thick, thin, fluffy, velvety, satin, bumpy,* or *prickly.*

Composition

The structure, arrangement, and organization of the parts into a relationship through the use of the elements of art.

Talk about the composition of children's work, describing the arrangement of parts as *balanced, symmetrical,* or *asymmetrical.*

When children have completed their projects, then teachers can describe the projects to them. Descriptions focusing on line, form, and color are very reinforcing to the children. When teachers take the time to actually think about an individual work, and find the words to describe it, children know adults really do care about them, their ideas, and their work (see Figure 7.4). On the other hand, children reject comments that are not individual or thoughtful. For example, when a teacher walked around the room as children were working with art materials and said to each, "Lovely, job!" "Good work!" "Lovely," one child looked up at her and said, "But you said that to everybody."

When commenting on children's work, avoid value judgments. Teachers who are concerned about developing children's knowledge of art avoid any reference to themselves. They do not say, "I just love it," "I like that color," or "I like the way you did ____." When teachers tell children what they like or love, children, who want to please teachers, will try to draw, paint, or construct in ways that will please the teacher. After all, the teacher has told them, "I really like ____."

Instead, effective teacher talk will be based on knowledge of the vocabulary and concepts of art. To help children meet the visual arts standards, teachers will need to model using the vocabulary of art and encourage children to use art talk in describing their artwork (see Figure 7.5).

Asking children to "tell me about it" has been overused in talking to children about their work. When asked to tell about his painting, one child said, "There's nothing to tell, it's just a pleasing design." Today's teachers, however, can get children to talk about their artwork by having them share their artwork with oth-

Figure 7.4. Assessing: Individual Structured Interview

- Set aside some time each day to talk with individual children about their artwork.

- Select a piece of work that has importance to a child. Children spend time and put forth a lot of effort on work that has special importance to them.

- Sit with the child and ask the child to
  * tell you about the painting, drawing, or sculpture
  * tell you what he or she was thinking of in creating a specific part, or how he or she did it
  * title his or her work
  * point out specific shapes, lines, colors, and textures.

- Record the child's responses, with date and place, in his or her portfolio.

- At the end of the year compare beginning work with current work.

Figure 7.5. Talking About Children's Artwork and the Work of Other Artists

- Make it a habit to use the vocabulary of art to describe children's work.

- Refer to children as artists.

- Ask children to think aloud about their work. Pose questions about the art process, such as, "How did you paint this?" and wait for a response (Althouse, Johnson, & Mitchell, 2003).

- Ask children to talk about experimenting with media—describe how clay feels to them, or what they can do or are doing with the clay. Scaffold the discussion by adding art vocabulary.

- Keep individual portfolios of children's work. Ask each child to select pieces to be included in the portfolio and tell why a piece of work is important to him or her.

- Document children's work by creating displays. Involve children in helping create the display, and selecting works they think should be displayed. Use the vocabulary of art to talk about the works displayed. Label the display for adults and for children. Incorporate art vocabulary into the labels.

- Describe the artwork found in children's books. Discuss how Eric Carle uses paper, scissors, and paste to create his illustrations; how Jerry Pinkney used pencil and watercolor to illustrate the book *Sam and the Tigers* (Lester, 2003); or how Denise Fleming uses pulp paper to create lush, rich illustrations of color and texture to illustrate her books.

- Display and talk about the work of well known artists. Prints of famous paintings can be provided for children. Ask children to give the painting a title. Have children tell why they chose the title, and then compare their title to the title the artist gave the painting.

ers (Epstein, 2001). For example, one teacher held a sharing time after art center time. Children were encouraged to show what they had created or built during center time, telling how they produced the work, what they were thinking of, and describing the work to the group. In this way, the teacher provided the time and arena to focus on talking about art.

THEATRE

Theatre is not often thought of as a part of the early childhood curriculum. Yet theatre has always been a part of the curriculum as children take part in social and pretend play. By providing opportunities, time, and props, teachers can help children achieve the theatre standards of *participating in sociodramatic playgroups* and *taking on roles of others in creative dramatics*. From these embryonic beginnings, more formal productions with sets, scripts, producers, actors, and audiences evolve during the primary grades.

From Pretend to Sociodramatic Play

Preschoolers are motivated to play as if they were another person, an animal, or an inanimate object. Psychoanalytic theories of play hold that children play "as if" in an attempt to understand the complex world in which they live. Observe young children to see this theory in action. A 3-year-old, watching llamas eating, raised and lowered her head as the llamas did, as if to understand more fully what she was seeing. After a haircut a boy picked up a block and tried to cut everyone's hair with his "shaver." Typically, after the birth of a new baby, preschoolers will pretend to be a baby, sucking on a pacifier, trying on baby clothes—all, perhaps, in an attempt to better understand babies.

From the beginnings of pretend play, sociodramatic play emerges. Sociodramatic play encompasses the features of pretend play but expands on pretend play with social and verbal interaction. Others and language are necessary to carry out sociodramatic play. At least two children, usually more, are needed to play as if they were a family getting ready for school, or a clerk and

Some hollow blocks and a blanket create a space for dramatic play.

customer at a store. And children need language to explain, negotiate, argue about, or command what the roles will be and who will assume them. (See Figure 7.6 for ways teachers can encourage sociodramatic play.)

Sociodramatic play is cognitive. Children seem to think aloud about their experiences as they try out different roles (Cooper & Dever, 2001). As they play, children gradually sort out reality from fantasy. They think aloud about their experiences, elaborating and rearranging what they know of the world. By experimenting with the various roles of the people in their home, school, and community, children come into contact with the needs and wishes of others. Through negotiation of roles during sociodramatic play, children slowly develop the idea that others have views that differ from theirs, and they learn to accommodate differing points of view.

Document children's cognitive growth and development through sociodramatic play. Take digital photos of children as they play, and record what they are saying, or note the problem they are solving. After sharing the photos with the children and their families, keep them in the children's portfolios as documentation of their learning.

Creative Dramatics

Creative dramatics are difficult for preschool children. Because of their preoperational thinking, some preschoolers have difficulty understanding the idea of acting. Even though 3- to 5-year-olds can play as if they were someone else, acting as a character in a story or a play is problematic. Moreover, preschoolers are active; they have trouble sitting still long enough to be an audience for others and waiting their turn to perform. Learning to take part in creative dramatics evolves from children's sociodramatic play. By kindergarten, children can begin to be involved in creative dramatics.

Figure 7.6. Encouraging Pretend and Sociodramatic Play

- Provide time for pretend and sociodramatic play from preschool through the early primary grades

- Select props that are reflective of children's experiences such as cooking tools from various cultures; for example, woks, chopsticks, wonton presses

- Offer clothing items that lend themselves to taking on fantasy as well as real roles. Pieces of lace curtains are good for playing king or queen, scarves for wicked witches.

So that children do not have to wait their turn, begin creative dramatics by involving everyone. To teach children to use their imaginations formally, start with pantomime. For example, ask children in a group to pretend they are holding a ball. Ask what size their ball is, what kind, color, and how they hold it. They can then bounce their pretend balls, and throw and catch each other's balls.

On another day, pair children and give them a task to pantomime, like setting a table together, baking a cake, or walking a dog. When familiar with just pretending, kindergarten and primary children can take on the part of a character. Select some poem or short story in which everyone can have a part. Good examples are nursery rhymes, such as Five Little Speckled Frogs or Humpty Dumpty, in which children can take turns playing Humpty Dumpty while all the others play the king's horses and men. (See Figure 7.7 for suggestions on including children with special needs in creative dramatics.)

Toward the end of kindergarten and in the primary grades children can put on plays to retell a story. When children are familiar with the idea of acting out a story, parts can be assigned, and children, taking on the part of the character, act out the story. In kindergarten teachers still need to narrate in order to keep the story moving along. Regardless, by taking the part of characters, children become familiar with the idea of story structure.

Once in the primary grades, children can put on entire plays. Stories with a number of characters, like *The Little Red Hen*, lend themselves to creative dramatics. Roles are assigned to some children, and others may design parts of the set using objects and materials in the classroom. Then roles can be exchanged, and the play put on again so every child has a turn. (See Figure 7.8 for an extended example of creative dramatics in a first-grade classroom.)

Figure 7.7. Including All Children in Creative Dramatics

- Children with physical disabilities can be incorporated into the act; a child in a wheelchair, for instance, could narrate parts of the play as well as act other roles.

- Shy children might hold up a prop or ring a bell at a given time, thus taking a less stressful part than a speaking role.

Figure 7.8. An Integrated Creative Dramatics Experience

The book *Journey Cake, Ho!* by Ruth Sawyer (1953), the Appalachian version of the Gingerbread Boy, was read and reread in one first-grade classroom. As the teacher read, children chimed in repeating familiar phrases such as "A bother and a pest, all work and no rest," and especially "Journey Cake, Ho! Journey Cake, Hi! Catch me and eat me as I roll by."

The teacher wrote some of the favorite phrases on a chart, and from time to time, as she ran her hand under the words, the children would read the phrases. Then the teacher asked children to take on the roll of the boy and cake, the cow and other animals. The children didn't run around the room, but stood and repeated the refrain, the child acting as the cow said, "At running I'll beat you, I'll catch you and eat you."

To culminate the experience, the children put on a play of the Journey Cake. They first painted a mural of hills and valleys, trees and ponds, on two pieces of brown wrapping paper joined together to make a large backdrop. Using sponges, the children painted the top of the paper blue to represent the sky, and bottom of the paper green to represent hills and valleys. Trees, ponds, houses, and barns were added. Then, taping the mural to the wall, children put on the play. One of the children announced the play, giving the title and author. The other children were assigned roles of people and animals (cows, ducks, and so on), with each child playing a role. Children acted out the play several times, changing roles so all children had a turn playing the boy, the cake, the little old woman, and the little old man.

To document children's work, digital photos were taken and children painted pictures of themselves acting out the play. Both the photos and paintings were made into books that children took turns taking home and reading to their families. A blank page at the end of the book allowed people who read the book to sign and comment on the children's work.

MUSIC

Since the beginnings of early childhood education in our nation when Froebel introduced music into the kindergarten curriculum, music has been integral to the early childhood curriculum. A wonderful joy, music sharpens and delights the senses as it fills the early childhood classroom. Teachers sing name songs to greet children, chant marches as children are on a field trip, and spontaneously lead children in song during work time. Throughout the day children naturally perform and respond to the fundamental music processes (see Figure 7.9).

Not only is music an integral part of the school day, music is intricately linked to children's growth and development. Children's responses to sound and rhythm are as natural as growth itself. As soon as children begin to walk, or even before, their entire bodies respond to sounds they hear. And music is integral to the curriculum as well. As another language for learning, for creative expression, music fosters children's thinking skills and abstract learning (see Figure 7.10).

Through music drawn from many cultures, traditions, and backgrounds, music unites humans. The diversity in today's classrooms provides students with distinctive learning advantages (CNEA, 1994). With music, children can "juxtapose unique elements of their individual cultural traditions with elements that have been embraced, incorporated, and transformed into a shared culture" (p. 10).

While music is a natural part of children's lives, in the curriculum it should be a carefully and thoughtfully planned experience (Achilles, 1999). Achieving the music standards means setting aside a special time each day for music designed to teach children to *listen to music, use rhythm instruments, become familiar with musical symbols and notes,* and *use their voices to sing individually and with a group.*

Listening to Music

Learning to listen involves perception and the organization of perceptual responses. Listening—one of the abilities infants possess at birth—develops as do all other skills, as children grow and mature. By 2 years of age or even before, children enjoy listening to songs sung by others or songs on CDs or video clips. Two- and 3-year-olds enjoy listening to music they make them-

Figure 7.9. Music Throughout the Day

- *Lighten a tense moment.* When things get out of hand, teachers can sing a soothing refrain, perhaps "Hush little baby, don't say a word," or "Love somebody, yes I do," to quiet things down. Even beginning to hum a familiar song, such as "Here We Are Together" leads children to quiet down and join in singing the song.

- *Ease transitions.* Singing songs that tell children it's time to clean up, get ready to go out to play, or come to a group meeting, eases moving from one activity to another.

Figure 7.10. Music as a Language for Learning

- *Auditory discrimination.* Children learn to listen to sounds, to distinguish between and among different sounds, a precursor to learning to hear sounds in words.

- *Social skills.* The importance of learning to work with a group, to be one with the group, cannot be underestimated. Musical activities give children the opportunity to be at one with the group. Children with special needs can be involved; singing with others or playing rhythm instruments helps them become important members of the groups.

- *Rhyming words.* The familiar rhyming phrases of songs sung many times enable children to develop the idea that words have similar ending sounds that are called rhymes.

- *Segmentation.* An important reading skill is being able to segment words, to know that words consists of parts. Singing songs that emphasize parts of words, such as "Lit-tle Pe-ter Rab-bit had a fly upon his nose" enables children to gain an understanding of segmentation.

- *Abstract thinking.* Music is abstract, so by participating in music, children are gaining experiences in abstract thinking.

- *Mathematics.* Music involves counting, pausing, phrasing, and patterns, all of which are a part of mathematics.

---

selves as they bang pots together or listen to their own voices. By 4 or 5, children will be able to pick out the sounds of specific instruments from a recording.

Throughout children's experiences with sounds, adults can acquaint them with the vocabulary of music. Children are first able to understand the concept of loudness and are able to distinguish loud from soft sounds. Next, children are able to distinguish duration from pitch. Still, 5-year-olds remain confused about the terms *high, loud,* and *fast; low, soft,* and *slow.* (See Figure 7.11 for definitions of the vocabulary of music.)

A carrel, built from a discarded cardboard box big enough to hold a table and a child or two, or a tent to crawl inside, or just a nook or corner separated from the rest of the room by a bookshelf, can serve as a listening area. Different sound makers can be categorized in baskets for children to use in the carrel. Bells, rattles, maracas, wood blocks, or actual instruments can be provided for children to make sounds.

Music draws from many cultures.

After a period of exploration, children can be asked to solve problems with the instruments. They might be asked to find and categorize the instruments that make a striking sound, those that make a prolonged ringing sound, and those that produce shorter, or smooth sounds.

In one classroom for 4-year-olds children studied musicians. Several of the children's parents played musical instruments in a community orchestra, and another parent taught instrumental music at a local high school. Drawing on the families as a resource, the teacher asked parents to visit the school and play their instruments. One parent played the violin as the children listened. She brought along practice violins and taught the children how to hold the bow and violin and play the violin. Surprisingly, the result was pleasing musical sounds. The parent taught the children how to use the bow to create sad and happy sounds, fast and slow sounds. Other parents did the same with a trumpet, drums, and a piano keyboard.

On another day, children listened to selections of instrumental pieces and were able to pick out the violins, drums, and other instruments. To document their work, the class made a book entitled "Musical Instruments." Children illustrated the book with pictures of different musical instruments and drawings to explain how sounds were produced.

Using Rhythm Instruments

Rhythm instruments have been a part of the early childhood curriculum since the beginnings of kindergarten in our nation. Both Patty Smith Hill and Anna Bryan, who pioneered early education in our nation, advocated the use of found objects as rhythm instruments to enable children to explore a number of sounds. With these instruments, children could form their own band.

Purchasing rhythm instruments is recommended today. After all, if teachers want children to play the instruments to make music, it makes sense to purchase good instruments. Triangles, rhythm sticks, bells, drums, a xylophone, and a set of tone blocks are probably essential. Be sure to purchase enough instruments so each child will be able to play in the rhythm band.

Teachers find that introducing one instrument at a time is productive. When children use one instrument at a time for a given purpose, they become familiar with the sounds the instrument can make and the potential uses of individual instruments.

Then children need to learn to keep time with the music. Teachers might begin with a familiar nursery rhyme or chant and have children clap the rhythm. Or children could play the pattern on a drum, with rhythm sticks, or on a tone block. Play a musical selection with a slow beat, and have children follow the slow beat clapping their hands, stomping their feet, or slapping their thighs. Then play a fast musical piece and do the same.

Figure 7.11. Using the Vocabulary of Music

Pitch

The key or keynote of a tune. Children associate the words *high* and *low* and *up* and *down* with position and place. The idea of high and low pitch are introduced. Use tone blocks or step bells, with the lowest pitch blocks to children's left and the highest pitch to their right.

Rhythm

The all-encompassing word used to describe the time-based or temporal components of music. *Beat, meter, duration,* and *tempo* are temporal terms. The words *fast* and *slow* are familiar to children, but they need to be introduced to the idea that the tempo of music is fast or slow.

Dynamics

The varying intensity of sound in a piece of music. Children are introduced to the idea that music can be loud or soft.

Timbre

The unique qualities of sound made by voices or instruments. Children can learn to identify instruments by recognizing the timbre of a specific instrument.

Mood

The interaction of music and emotion. Children can talk about what a particular piece of music makes them feel.

Use three or four rhythm instruments children are familiar with. Have one child turn his or her back, while another selects and plays one instrument and places it back on a table. Have the child turn around and pick out the instrument that was played.

Start a rhythm band with children playing just one or two instruments, and work up to a full rhythm band. Record children's playing so they can step back and listen to their band.

Singing

Who hasn't heard children chanting and singing as they play? "Skip, skip, skip, up and down, up and down," sings the toddler. "Sandy, sandy, mandy, mandy," chants the preschooler. In the typical minor third (sol-mi), the melodic, repetitive chants of children are heard around the world. Two- and 3-year-olds are responsive to hearing teachers sing or repeat these simple chants back to them.

Two- and 3-year-olds also enjoy singing along with familiar finger plays and chants. Five Little Blackbirds, Little Chickadees, Open Shut Them—all of these old favorites are new and enchanting to children as they gradually sing along and learn the words of the entire song. By the time children are 4 years old, they'll enjoy songs about things close to them, as well as the same old familiar favorites. Five-year-olds are more able to actually carry a tune, even though they still have a limited singing range. Songs that have directional melodies, that go up and then down, seem well suited to 5-year-olds.

Children can be introduced to the symbols of music. On a chart a teacher can write the notes and words of best loved songs. Using her hand to sweep under the notes and words, the teacher guides the children to follow along by singing the song. It isn't expected that

Clapping and singing together is a pleasure.

children will learn to read music, only to become familiar with the notation and symbols of music.

DANCE

Moving and dancing to music require *the ability to control and execute rhythmic movements* and then the *abilities to listen to music, execute rhythmic movements, and put the two together*. Moving to music is a complex process. Children must first have knowledge of different musical sounds, and then be able to conceptualize and execute movements to match these sounds. Obviously, these skills develop gradually and begin with children learning to control large muscles.

Accompanying children's movements with a drumbeat, perhaps as children are jumping and running out of doors, is a beginning step in teaching children to control movements and then put them together to music. After children hear their steps in a drumbeat, they'll begin experimenting. Teachers might ask children to name what parts of their body made stomping sounds, or which parts they used to jump, sway, or glide across the room. One teacher followed children's movements with drumbeats as they played with large beach balls. Children dribbled the balls, held onto them before bouncing them, and rolled them back and forth.

Songs about planes or trains, birds flying, or people marching lead children to moving as if they were the birds, trains, or marchers. Short piano selections can be played, and children encouraged to move, or dance, to the music. They might move by themselves, or chose a partner or group to dance with. Taking digital photos or videos of children moving, and then, as they view these, talking about what they were doing, thinking, and how they moved, helps children understand the idea of dancing to music. Only with experience and maturity will children learn to move or dance to musical selections.

IN SUMMARY

- The arts—visual arts, music, theatre, and dance—were identified in Goals 2000 as core subject matter. All children should develop competency in the arts.
- The arts, separate and valid content areas in themselves, are integral to the entire curriculum. The arts contribute to the development of various cognitive skills, such as creative thinking and problem-solving skills.
- Visual arts include a wide range of media, tools, and techniques and are connected to most parts of the curriculum. Learning to talk about art enhances language learning and reading as well as art ability.

- Theatre, which seems distant from young children's lives, begins with children's pretend and sociodramatic play and moves on to informal dramatics and then more formal dramatic plays. Children use dramatic play to understand their experiences in the world.
- Music permeates the entire school day. Learning to listen to music, use rhythm instruments, and sing have long been a part of all good programs for young children.
- Dance starts with children's natural physical responses to sound and rhythm. But dance is a complex activity requiring musical knowledge and good control of physical movements.

SAMPLE INVESTIGATION: CHILDREN STUDY THEIR PLAY YARD

The Visual Arts

Being out of doors gives children another type of motivation for expressing their ideas, feelings, and experiences through art. Further, creating visual arts out of doors offers children the opportunity to use art materials in expanded ways.

Selected standards

Master a variety of art media.
Express ideas through the visual arts.
Recognize and talk about the concepts of art.

Activities

Toddlers (two–three years old)

- Give children the opportunity to scribble and use large muscles as they paint outdoors. Attach large sheets of mural paper to the play yard fence or tape paper to a concrete wall. Paints can be provided in an old six-pack of discarded juice cans along with large sponge brushes. Children are free to come and paint, run off, and come back and paint some more. The point is for children to experience the freedom of painting large outdoors.

Preschoolers (three–four years old)

- Place large paper, staplers, tape, and glue on a table out of doors. Children gather leaves, acorns, and other objects found on the play yard and create a nature collage.
- Bring a variety of large boxes and joining materials (tape, staplers, and so on) out of doors. Children move the boxes to construct a fort, truck, boat, or house.

Kindergarten children (four–five years old)

- Explore texture with the children. With the children, observe the play yard to find things that are rough or smooth. Give children large crayons and pieces of paper and show them how to make rubbings. The teacher could place the paper on the sidewalk and rub the crayon over the paper. Note the roughness of the sidewalk and the rough-looking rubbing. Other rubbings could be made of the tires on wheeled toys, tree trunks, wooden slats, and the smooth slide.
- Back in the classroom, talk about the rubbings and name the surfaces of the yard. Categorize the rubbings on a chart:

Concrete Driveway	Smooth
Tree	Rough
Pebbled Walk	Bumpy
Slide	Smooth

- On another day look for lines on the play yard. Give children clipboards with several sheets of paper attached along with markers. Ask them to draw play equipment using lines. They might draw the slide with wavy lines and the steps leading to the slide

A new piece of play yard equipment motivated children's drawings.

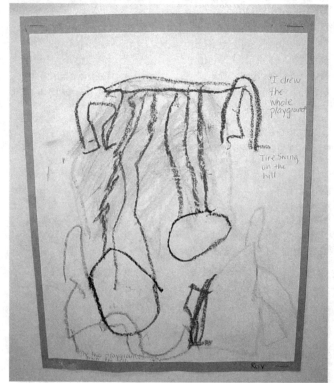

with straight lines. Or they could draw any other lines found on the play yard.

Assessing Children's Learning

Observe

- Record the language of the visual arts that children use as they discuss their own drawings and paintings or the artwork of others.

Interview

- Ask individual children to tell you about their drawings or paintings. Record instances of children using the vocabulary of texture or lines.
- Ask children to identify their work and the work of others. They may be able to start comparing and contrasting their work with that of others (e.g., "I always use red, Shawna likes green").

CHAPTER 8

Integrating the Language and Literacy Standards

Today's pressures for accountability places the spotlight on language and literacy, including reading and writing. Research is clear: Children with foundational skills of listening and speaking, familiarity with print and books, knowledge of story structure and the purposes of writing are those who will benefit most from reading instruction, learn to read sooner, and read better than children without these skills (Strickland & Morrow, 2000; Whitehurst & Longman, 1998).

With the language and literacy standards to guide them, teachers of young children will be able to plan and implement programs designed to foster children's language and literacy learning. Language learning and learning to read and write require mastery of a number of diverse skills and knowledge. These skills are so tightly integrated with each other that it's difficult to separate them into categories. For example, the skills of listening and speaking are difficult to separate, as are the skills involved in learning what print means and being able to write and read it.

Just as the language and literacy standards are tightly integrated with each other, language learning simply cannot be separated out from the school day. Language learning is a vital part of everything that takes place in good schools for young children. (For example, see the "Sample Investigation" at the end of the chapter.) The standards, which differentiate language and literacy skills, help teachers to think of language learning as a separate entity. By identifying and delineating language and literacy skills, the standards provide teachers with the framework they need to ensure that all children will be prepared to read and achieve academic success.

The goals of this chapter are to

- Present the language and literacy standards
- Describe language and literacy environments of good schools for young children

- Discuss the development of phonemic awareness
- Illustrate the Language Experience Approach as a method of providing documentation for experiential learning and teaching concepts of print and specific language skills
- Describe the importance of vocabulary learning and how to promote children's vocabulary learning through dialogical book reading and knowledge of story structure
- Demonstrate how writing emerges and describe the relationship between writing, reading, and phonemic awareness

THE LANGUAGE AND LITERACY STANDARDS

The language and literacy standards that follow should be considered as examples of those that may be presented to teachers. I derived these standards from the *Standards for the English Language Arts* (NCTE/IRA, 2003) and *Reading and Writing Grade by Grade: Primary Literacy Standards* (New Standards, 1999).

For the purposes of this book it was necessary to select those standards representing the major ideas of language and literacy, including reading and writing. Further, as the standards documents were written for children from K–4, 5–8, and the secondary grades, only standards pertaining to young children was selected. The selection of the following standards was guided by the *Pre-K Standards* of CTB/McGraw-Hill (2002) and McREL's *Content Knowledge: A Compendium of Standards and Benchmarks for K–12 Education* (Kendall & Marzano, 2004).

The language and literacy standards are both declarative—identifying the content children are to learn —and procedural—describing what children will be able to do.

1. Listening. Children will:
    1.a. Identify sounds in their environment
    1.b. Create sounds by singing and music making
    1.c. Listen and speak with attention
    1.d. Listen for pleasure
    1.e. Develop phonemic awareness
    1.f. Identify letter-sound relationships
2. Speaking. Children will:
    2.a. Develop conversation skills with peers and adults
    2.b. Speak in small groups and the whole class
    2.c. Use vocabulary introduced through explicit experiences or book reading
    2.d. Ask and answer questions
    2.e. Use increasingly complex sentence structure
3. Reading. Children will:
    3.a. Recognize that written symbols and print convey meaning
    3.b. Increase receptive and expressive vocabulary
    3.c. Develop book familiarity
    3.d. Interact in read-alouds
    3.e. Develop an understanding of story structure
    3.f. Increase word-decoding skills
4. Writing. Children will:
    4.a. Recognize graphemes—the letters of the alphabet
    4.b. Engage in pencil/paper/drawing/painting activities
    4.c. Incorporate print into drawings
    4.d. Express ideas through writing using emergent spelling and progress to conventional spelling
    4.e. Gain meaning by reading their own writing and that of others

A LANGUAGE-RICH ENVIRONMENT

Children naturally learn language and literacy skills as they live (Barbarin, 2002; NCR, 2001b). Listening, babbling, saying one-word sentences, children learn language. Children also naturally learn literacy skills, if they experience environments rich in language, full of the spoken and written word.

What follows is a description of a high-quality early educational environment that is purposefully rich in language and literacy. Consider the various components. The environment is structured in ways that make children fall in love with language, books, and writing. First, children are encouraged to talk with others about what they are doing and thinking. Child-adult talk is viewed as especially important. Learning to listen, not only to each other, but to distinguish between environmental sounds and the sounds of letters, is fostered. Experiences are planned to develop pho-

nemic awareness, so children can break the print-code meaning. (See Figure 8.1 for definitions of language terms.)

In good schools for young children, experiences are designed to foster children's vocabulary learning. Research shows that the more words children know, the better readers they will become (Wasik, Bond, & Hindman, 2001). Through projects or investigations, children become acquainted with words new to them and incorporate these into their vocabulary.

Vocabulary is learned and used as children talk with each other and adults about what they are doing. Opportunities are provided for children to dictate their ideas and express them through their own writing, inventing spelling as they go. Stories children write are read to each other and to the group. Copies are made so children and families can enjoy reading children's narratives.

A high-quality environment is filled with purposeful print. There are charts and signs to read informing children of something new, something to do, or something to observe. Writing is encouraged throughout the

Figure 8.1. Useful Definitions

___

Phonemic Awareness

The understanding that speech consists of a series of written sounds. This awareness is a powerful predictor of children's later reading achievement (Whitehurst & Longman, 1998).

Phonics

The relationship between letters and sounds that are taught to give children a tool to analyze and pronounce words new to them.

Onset

The letter pattern in a syllable that includes any consonants before a vowel.

Rime

The letter pattern in a syllable that includes the vowel and any consonants that follow. Rimes may also be called *word families* or *phonograms*. A *rime* is not the same thing as a *rhyme*, which may be defined as two or more words that end with the same sound.

Reading

The process of bringing meaning to the printed word; to observe and understand the meaning of the printed word and be able to say it aloud.

___

room. Paper and markers are a part of each area or center of the room. For example, in the housekeeping area children find notebooks to write in, calendars to fill in, note pads and pencils to make notes on, and receipt books to fill in. A writing center holds blank books and all kinds of markers and models of print encouraging children to write.

Just as print is found throughout the room, so are books. There is a well-equipped book area, but books to consult are placed with the blocks and in the dramatic play, science, and other areas of the room. Book reading takes place daily. Children and adults read individually, and children read to one another. Story time and read-alouds are deliberately planned to foster children's listening, reading, and writing skills.

Music and art, key to language and literacy learning, are integral. Art and music are other languages for learning. Children learn to express their ideas using the symbol systems of the visual and musical arts.

Children just learning English will find safety in singing or chanting English words in a group. Through music, they can practice their English without being singled out. Creating through the visual arts gives children just learning English another mode of expression.

In good schools for young children, language and literacy flourish. Language is so fundamental to learning and teaching that it may seem unnecessary to focus on language or literacy learning. Yet by applying the language standards to daily, ongoing language experiences, teachers will be able to refine and perfect what they are already doing, increasing and enriching children's opportunities to become successful readers and learners.

Music and language learning go hand in hand.

LISTENING, SPEAKING, AND ESTABLISHING PRINT-SOUND CORRESPONDENCE

Listening and Speaking

The "interrelated and whole" (NCTE/IRA, 2003) language standards assume that the curriculum will also be whole and integrated. Experiential learning, through projects, themes, or units, offers children a multitude of integrated experiences designed to refine and develop their listening and speaking skills. Through integrated language experiences children should achieve the first two sets of language and literacy standards, those of *listening* and *speaking*.

Experiences demand listening and give children not only something to talk, read, and write about, but the purpose for doing so. Experiences that call for listening skills are easily incorporated into typical themes. During a study of birds common to the school yard children were asked to observe the body parts responsible for making the sound, to distinguish between different birds' songs and calls, and to hypothesize if there was a reason for the different calls. Were the sounds of a bird's calls happy, frightened, beautiful, or angry? Another group studying animals charted the sounds their classroom pets made, including no sounds at all in the case of fish and the mealworms they were observing.

Children's abilities to discriminate between and among environmental sounds has also been extended through a study of toys. After finding toys that made sounds, the group identified the types of sounds. Some sounds were loud and screechy, others were soft and musical. The source of sounds, batteries in the case of some toy cars and dolls, were discovered and discussed. The study ended with children finding out which of a group of toys made the loudest sound. They did so by having children take turns standing in the front of the room and operating the toy to make a sound, while the rest were in the back of the room with their backs to the sound producer. The children in the back of the room paired up sharing clipboards to record the source of the sounds they could hear. Later the group graphed the sounds that could be heard when they were far from the source.

The ultimate goal, however, is to be able to listen attentively, with a purpose, and respond appropriately. That's why teachers purposefully engage children in talking about what they are doing. Talking about something of interest to the child and to the adult creates a bond and increases children's listening and speaking skills. (See Figure 8.2 for ways to help children just learning English develop these language skills.)

As teachers listen to children, they expand on what the children are saying. This seems to foster children's

The ultimate goal is to learn to listen with purpose.

listening and oral language skills, and increases their vocabulary. For example, when a child says, "Look—me painting," the teacher might respond, "Jeanna, you are painting with red and blue paints." A teacher might respond to a child who says, "Me want," by saying "Yes, you want more cookies now, but we need to put these away for later." Or to a child who says "Doggie barking," "Yes, the dog is barking, but he won't bite you."

While talking with children about what they are doing, adults give children the names of things. One teacher, observing children working with sand, handed one a sieve. She said, "Try this sieve. Hold the handle [pointing to the handle], and now fill the cup with sand. Watch what happens to the sand when you shake it over the sieve."

Figure 8.2. Language Skills for Children Just Learning English

To help children just learning English develop their language skills, they should be given the opportunities to

- Enter into play and work with other children, using both their home language and English
- Increase their vocabulary of nouns, naming familiar objects in both their home language and English
- Take part in group songs, chants, and poetry
- Recite home language and English poems and songs on tape, video clips, or CDs
- Teach words in their home language to others in the group
- Greet others in both their home language and English

In addition to naming items and their parts, teachers can use words that describe what children are doing. "Your hand moved quickly across the paper," one teacher told a scribbler scribbling away. She told another child who was jumping to some music, "Your feet land so softly, just like leaves gently falling from a tree."

Teachers encourage children to use language to solve problems. If children spill paint, teachers help them put words to the cleanup process. "What should you do? You take this paper and start wiping here. I'll get the sponge." Or to a child whose pant leg was caught in a trike wheel, "What should we do? Let's try moving the bike backward; maybe that will help." Questioning fosters thinking and problem solving when teachers ask children, "What will happen if . . . ," "How can you . . . ," "What would you do to . . . ," or "How does this work?"

In summary, listening and speaking skills are interwoven. As children learn to listen, they learn to speak. In good schools for young children speech is fostered by teachers in the following ways:

- Giving children something to talk about—investigations with their world through project and thematic learning, problems to solve
- Really listening to children talk and responding to what they say—if a child says, "Wood hard," expanding and extending the statement, talking about the wood and its hardness
- Encouraging children to ask questions during book reading
- Providing opportunities for children to speak in front of the class—for instance, asking children to tell how they made something or accomplished a task
- Encouraging children to contribute to language experience stories
- Asking children to take part in creative dramatics, taking on the roles of others
- Having children read to others—either books that are familiar to them or books they've written
- Giving children opportunities to record and listen to their voices—singing, chanting, or reading books

Developing Phonemic Awareness

Phonemic awareness goes hand in hand with learning to listen and speak. At the same time children are learning to hear, recognize, and segment environmental sounds, they are learning phonemes. *Phonemes* are the minimal sound units represented by the written language (Adams, 1990). Children's awareness that words are made up of a number of sounds, or phonemes, is believed to be a critical skill. Research suggests that children's phonemic awareness is a powerful predicator of later reading success (Adams, 1990).

Because English is based on the alphabetic principle—the spoken word maps onto the written word—children who understand that words are made of sounds seem to have an easier time learning the letter-sound relationship (Vacca & Vacca, 2003). Without phonemic awareness, children could learn letter-sound relationships, but would not be able to use this knowledge to read or spell words new to them.

Phonemic awareness is comprised of four skills:

1. *Rhyming*—being able to recognize ending sounds that are alike in words
2. *Segmenting beginning and ending sounds in words*—being able to recognize and name the sounds at the beginning and ending of words
3. *Segmenting separate sounds in a word*—being able to separate the "ing" in *coming*, or the "art" in *cart*.
4. *Blending*—being able to combine letter sounds to make words. Given the sounds of the letters /c/a/r/ the child would say "car."

How do children learn phonemic awareness? By listening to poems and playing with language! Poems, often forgotten in today's curriculum, are a joyous, wonder-filled, beautiful way to introduce children to

Children fall in love with language.

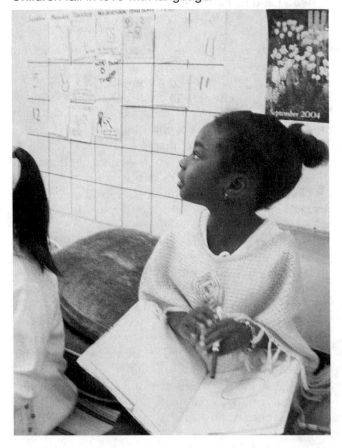

the sounds and patterns of their language and meet any number of language standards, especially those revolving around phonemic awareness.

Hearing poetry throughout the day helps children focus on the sounds and patterns of their language. Children hear the spoken word as a steady stream of sounds. At some point in time, before or during first grade, children must be able to attend to the separate sounds of speech, to consciously notice the parts of words, whole words, and the sentences they make. Children who realize that words are made of phonemes, a sequence of sounds, are better able to understand the letter-sound relationship. A steady diet of poetry is one way for children to learn to focus and attend to the individual sounds of speech. By listening to and reciting poems, children gain knowledge of standards revolving around knowledge of (1) rhyme and rimes; (2) blending, and (3) segmentation.

Rhyme and rimes. A *rhyme* may be defined as two or more words that end with the same sound, whether or not they are spelled alike. *Fear* and *tear* are spelled alike, but *fear* and *deer* are examples of rhymes that end with the same sound but are not spelled the same. A *rime*, on the other hand, is the part of the letter pattern in a word that includes the vowel and any consonants that follow. Examples of rimes are the *ell* in *bell* and *sell*, the *ee* in *see* and *bee*, and the *ear* in *fear* and *tear*. The beginning letter, or *onset*, changes in words that share a rime, but the ending is the same. Rimes are also called *phonograms* or *word families*.

Knowledge or awareness of rimes and onsets may be the key to helping children develop phonemic awareness (Adams, 1990). Awareness of rhyme seems to develop relatively early and easily. By making them a focus of explicit instruction, teachers may be able to help children isolate and recognize phonemes more easily. With knowledge of rimes and onsets children are able to decode words new to them. A child was able to decode the word *still* by comparing it with the word *bill*. Wylie and Durrell (1970) pointed out that with knowledge of a set of 37 common and familiar rimes, such as *ack*, *ail*, *est*, *ice*, *ink*, and *ight*, children would be able to read nearly 500 words found in typical primary-level reading books.

Not only can teachers sing, chant, and recite poetry all through every day, but they can make onsets and rimes explicit. Children can clap to words that rhyme, or teachers can pause in reading or reciting a poem for children to fill in the rhyming word. Visually, rhymes and rimes can also be made explicit. It seems that being able to see onsets and rimes helps children recognize onsets and rimes aurally. Charts can be made of favorite poems and rhyming words in them identified. Rimes might be underlined and onsets identified. Games can be played to identify onsets and rimes.

Adams (1990) cautions that teaching onsets and rimes can be overdone and misused. Rather than providing children with meaningless text like "a hat on a mat," research suggests that children should be engaged in

• Games and activities involving nursery rhymes
• Listening to rhymed poetry and stories
• Producing rhyme and poetry
• Visual isolation of onsets and rimes

Beginning sounds. Hearing an isolated sound is difficult, not just for young children, but for adults as well. We are so used to hearing whole streams of words that we do not consciously focus on the first sounds of words. Although sensitivity to rhyme seems to develop early and relatively easily, sensitivity to onsets or alliteration does not.

Exposing children to poems that include *alliteration*—repetition of the initial sound of a word in one or more closely following words—is one technique used to foster children's awareness of initial sounds. Some classic children's poems that include alliteration are the following:

Autumn Fires, *sing a song of seasons* (Stevenson, 1923)
Silver, *slowly, silently,* now the moon, (de la Mare, 1961)
Travel, *camel caravan* (Stevenson, 1923).

Familiar tongue twisters and nursery rhymes also can be used to foster children's awareness of alliteration.

Peter Piper picked a peck of pickled peppers.
How much wood could a wood chuck chuck?
She sells sea shells by the sea shore.
Sing a song of six pence.

Isolating initial phonemes and visually displaying these may help children with the difficult task of recognizing beginning sounds of words. Engaging the children in games and activities with initial sounds may also be useful.

Syllabication. Being able to identify sounds of parts of words involves syllabication. A *syllable* is a vowel or a cluster of letters containing a vowel and pronounced as a unit. Being able to break words into syllables is critical for decoding them and is believed to be a link between awareness of rhyme and awareness of individual phonemes.

Selecting poetry, songs, and chants that accent the syllables in words may enable children to develop awareness of syllabication. Clapping and dancing to syllabic rhythms has been found useful as well (Adams, 1990). Play with puppets who speak only in syllables and other games have been found to promote children's awareness of syllabication.

Blending. Learning tongue twisters might be one way for children to gain an understanding of blending individual sounds to make words. Children enjoy the challenge and fun of saying "She sells sea shells by the sea shore," or making up their own tongue twisters: "Bobby bounces blue balls on the blackboard." "Fred frets over freaky stories." Write tongue twisters on a chart. Underline and say the blending sounds.

READING: BRINGING MEANING TO THE PRINTED WORD

The definition of *reading* is to bring meaning to the printed word. Children can recognize letters and their sounds and pronounce words, but unless the words they pronounce have meaning, children are not reading.

The third set of standards revolve around children learning vocabulary in order to *bring meaning to the printed word*. Preparing children to learn to read means fostering children's vocabulary (Barbarin, 2002). There is a direct relationship between the number of words children understand and can use and their ability to read. The greater the children's vocabulary, the greater their reading achievement.

The Language Experience Approach

Years ago the language experience approach (LEA) to beginning reading was popular. Stemming from Dewey's (1944) theories of education, the LEA provided for integrating language learning through children's direct experiences with their world. During the 1960s and 1970s LEA was popular because it was based on the principle that thought and language are interdependent (Piaget, 1969; Vygotsky, 1986). Because it revolved around the whole, the LEA was a precursor to the whole word approach to beginning reading (Russell, 1970). The approach was largely replaced by programs of guided reading and writing and invented spelling. The idea behind the LEA is sequential:

• Children think about their experiences.
• What children think can be expressed orally.
• What children talk about can be written.
• What is written can be read.

By dictating their thoughts or feelings about an experience to the teacher, children see their spoken words being transcribed in writing and read back to them. In doing so, children learn to break the "print code," understand the conventions of print, develop receptive and expressive vocabulary, learn to listen and to speak to others, learn the use of specific language conventions such as capitals and punctuation, as well as learn letter names and sounds.

Revisiting the LEA is appropriate today for several reasons. First, we know that language learning is a shared activity. Learning to talk, listen, read and write takes place within a group of learners (Hawkins, 2004). The LEA provides the social interaction within a community necessary for language learning.

Then too, the LEA is an integral part of children's projects, investigations, and thematic learning. The language experience chart, individual stories, or individual books and class books that result from the language experience approach serve to document children's learning. By displaying charts and children's dictated stories, teachers document children's learning and communicate with others (see Figure 8.3).

Figure 8.3. Making the Home-School Connection (Language and Literacy)

Copy experience charts. Compile the charts into booklets, such as "Our September Experiences." Make a booklet of charts for each child to take home. Add a note explaining that the children dictated sentences about their experiences.

Common group experiences embedded in project learning are the beginning of the LEA. Any common experience, whether going on a visit to the fire station or observing the behavior of mealworms, can be used. Before the experience children listen to one another as they talk about what they already know about the topic and what they want to learn. The teacher writes children's responses on a chart. These responses are read back to the children. They can later be organized into a book; for example, "What We Know About Firefighters."

Or children could be asked to tell what they want to know about firefighters or whatever else they are studying. Their questions are written on a tagboard chart. If the group is going to do fieldwork, the chart can be cut apart with each child or teams of children in charge of asking the question they have in their hands.

After the study is complete, children dictate another chart entitled "What We Learned About Firefighters." This chart as well can be made into a class book with children contributing illustrations to match the written words.

Spontaneous events can lead to writing a group experience chart. After a light spring rain one group saw a nearly fully formed rainbow in the distance. The teacher quickly brought markers and paper to the play

yard so children could sketch the rainbow. When they could no longer see the rainbow, the children met as a group, and the teacher wrote their dictation of a story they entitled "Rainbow at Play." Again, a book was created from the chart with different children contributing illustrations. (See Figure 8.4.)

A language experience chart or story holds deep personal meaning to children because it stems from their actual experiences. The charts are controlled by children's own vocabulary and reflect their ideas, their knowledge, and their emotions. Because they do so, language experience charts and stories are useful in explicit teaching of conventions of language.

First, charts are read back to the children. As a teacher writes children's words on a chart, she or he reads them aloud. When a sentence or part is complete, with a hand sweeping under the words, the teacher reads the chart again. The children join in as parts of the chart are reread to find out what the group has written, if they included a specific point, or to determine what still needs to be written. When the chart is complete, it is read again, with children joining in. Individual children can be asked to read parts of the chart or the entire chart.

Implementing the LEA as a part of children's projects or thematic learning not only offers children multiple opportunities to increase their receptive and expressive vocabulary, but can help children fulfill nearly every language and literacy standard of learning (see Figure 8.5).

The teacher can refer to the complete sets of language and literacy standards and use the language ex-

Figure 8.4. Examples of Topics for Group Language Experience Charts

---

All About Reptiles (following a study of reptiles common to the area)

When We Were Babies (following a study of babies)

Our Butterflies (following a study of butterflies)

Fun in the Sun (dictated during the hottest days of summer)

Rainbow Ice (dictated after the teacher gave children ice cubes and food coloring to experiment with)

What We Learned About . . . . (to sum up what the group learned about a given topic)

The History of Our Kindergarten (at the end of the school, with each child contributing what he or she liked best while in kindergarten)

Figure 8.5. The Language Experience Approach—
What Children Learn

- Spoken words have a written counterpart.

- Words are made of rows of letters.

- Words are separated from each other by a wider space than the space between letters.

- The word that begins a sentence is capitalized. Names are capitalized as well.

- Sentences are made of words.

- Writing goes from left to right.

perience chart to foster children's learning of the delineated knowledge and skills as illustrated by the following examples:

- *We read from left to right.* Use one hand to demonstrate the left to right sweep as the children read the chart aloud.
- *The names of letters.* Have children find how many times the letter *c*, or any other letter, appears in a sentence. Ask them to frame the letter with their hands.
- *Punctuation marks.* Ask children to frame, using their hands or a paper frame, periods, question marks, commas, and so on.
- *Phonemic awareness, identifying beginning sounds of words.* Ask children to find words on the chart that begin with the same sound.
- *Phonemic awareness, identifying ending sounds of words.* Ask children to find words on the chart that end with the phonograms *in, ate, an, on,* and so on.
- *Sight words.* Have children find words they know, or count the number of times a specific word, such as *ball, balloon, was, happy,* and so on, appear on the chart.
- *The concept of sentences and words.* Ask children to find the longest and shortest words and sentences.
- *Words carry meaning.* Ask children to find the sentence that tells what they saw at the farm or how the pumpkin felt, the phrase that tells where we went, and so on.

Dialogical Book Reading

Children learn vocabulary, not only through firsthand experiences of conducting investigations and studying their world, but also through interaction with books. Dialogical book reading, or interactive book reading, gives teachers opportunities to build children's knowledge of specific words, which they may or may not use as they experience their world.

Thought to be the single most important activity for building reading success (Vacca & Vacca, 2003), every teacher, every day, everywhere, reads books to children. The already language-rich learning experience of reading books to children can be made even more valuable when standards guide the activity. Increasing their dialogical, or interactive, book-reading strategies will enable teachers to help children achieve numerous language and literacy standards while enriching and extending their learning.

Dialogical book reading encourages children to interact, cognitively and verbally with the story being read, the teacher, and other children (Vacca & Vacca, 2003). Teachers who involve children in higher order thinking through interactive reading seem to promote greater reading growth among students.

Dialogical book reading begins with teachers' identifying specific instructional goals and strategies for a book-reading activity. Teachers will want to consult the standards they are working with and use these to determine goals for interactive reading. They may also develop goals from their own observations and identification of children's needs.

The major goal of dialogical book reading is to engage children cognitively in the reading activity (Taylor & Pearson, 2003). When children are thinking about what they are listening to, they are developing

- Attentive or intentional listening skills
- Vocabulary
- Strategies for using their background knowledge as they think about what they are hearing read
- The ability to use semantic or syntactic cues
- An understanding of the reading process as thinking with text (Vacca & Vacca, 2003)
- The ability to reflect on the reading and apply their own ideas
- Strategies for decoding words
- Self-regulation

Before reading, teachers carefully select books to read aloud. Again, using the standards as a guide, teachers read through the book not only to familiarize themselves but to identify the language and reading skills they want to introduce while reading the book. If their goal is to fulfill the standard revolving around vocabulary building, teachers might identify one or two words they will focus on during the book reading. If they want children to learn to use clues from the book, its illustrations, or background knowledge to bring meaning to the text, teachers will list a few predictive or problem-solving questions to ask while reading the book. Or if the goal is to teach children strategies for decoding words new to them, then teachers would plan to show children words and talk about beginning and ending sounds of the words, parts of the word they already know, and so on.

To start a dialogical book-reading session, teachers read the title, the name of the author and perhaps illustrator of the book, making sure to use the words *title* and *author*. Teachers might show children the cover and ask them to predict what the story might be about, or a teacher might think aloud, "I wonder what this story is about. I see a little boy with a pair of goggles in his hand. I think this book is about goggles." Either way, teachers are involving children in thinking ahead—imagining and hypothesizing.

During the reading of the book, teachers continue thinking aloud and asking children to predict (What do you think will happen now?), draw conclusions (Why did she do that? How do you think he felt?), or relate their past experiences to the text (Have you ever . . . ? When did you feel like . . . ? What would you do?).

After the reading, teachers guide discussions about key ideas, asking children to tell about their favorite parts of the story, those that frightened them or made them happy. Teachers ask children to relate the story to their own lives: "How would you have felt if . . . ?" "Have you ever thought there was a monster in your closet?" "What would you have done . . . ?"

Developing word skills. As noted above, specific skills can be taught through read-alouds. Writing sentences or words from the book on a chart can draw children's attention to specific skills. If a teacher's goal is to teach children to recognize beginning sounds of words, she might list a couple of words on a chart from the book—*cake, cook, candle*—asking how these are alike and different. Going through parts of the book again, she can encourage children to find these words, and others that begin with the hard *c*.

Word families, or phonograms, found in the book could be listed on a chart. "Good night Mr. Pup, I'll see you in the morning when the sun comes up" (B. Martin, 1969), reads the teacher and asks, "Which words sound alike or end with rimes?" She then writes *pup* and *up* on a chart and encourages children to think of other words that rhyme with pup, or that end with the same phonogram.

Big books are useful in teaching sight vocabulary. If big books are not available, teachers can write sections of the book on a chart. Using the *cloze* method (post-it notes serve as paper flaps to cover specific words), children read the text and use context cues to tell what is under the flap. With big books or charts, children could frame, with their hands or a paper frame, specific words or all the words that

Begin alike

End with the same rimes or phonograms

Rhyme, but do not end with the same rime

Tell you to be worried, happy, sad, surprised, or make you laugh

See Figure 8.6 for teaching strategies to use interactive book reading with children just beginning to learn English.

Understanding story structure. Dialogical readings are useful in teaching children story structure. Knowledge of story structure is a strong predictor of reading success. Children who are familiar with stories, who can tell personal stories, or retell stories, are those who seem to be good readers (Neuman, Copple, & Bredekamp, 2000). It may be that knowledge of setting and understanding characters and their intentions, personalities, and characteristics gives children the foundation of meaning they need to make sense of a text. With knowledge of story plot, themes, and so on, children may be better able to use contextual cues to figure out and read words new to them.

Selecting narrative books, books that tell a story, teachers can use dialogical strategies to teach children story form. As noted earlier, while reading the cover teachers might ask children to predict where the story will take place, what events will occur, and the general theme of the story. The beginning and ending of the story can be identified, and questions can be asked about characters and plots during the reading of the story.

Questions about characters lead children to thinking about the intentions and personalities of the main characters in the story:

Figure 8.6. Dialogical Reading for Children Just Learning English

The following teaching strategies may be used in interactive book reading to help children just learning English:

- Write signs, labels, and charts in children's home language and English.

- Take time to talk with each individual child about his or her experiences.

- Find books, perhaps at the local library or from families, written in children's home language.

- Build security with private book readings with one or two children who speak the same language.

- Repeat readings of predictable texts in English.

Children learn story structure.

Do you think she is honest? Would you like her for a friend?

How do you think Sal is going to feel? Why do you think he did that?

Who would you like to be? Which character would you like as a friend and why?

Discussion of the setting takes place. Teachers focus children's attention on the setting, relating it to the story theme or plot. Teachers might ask:

Is this a pretend place or a real place? What will happen here?

Would you like to live here? Why do think he is wearing a big coat, mittens, and boots?

Events are predicted and discussed. Children are asked to think ahead by predicting what will happen next and why. Or children can be asked to predict what will happen after the story is over. By doing so they are developing their own ideas of story structure. For example:

What will Peter in *The Snowy Day* (Keats, 1996) do when it isn't snowing?

Where will Goldilocks take a walk tomorrow?

Where will the Gingerbread Boy live when he stops running?

What will Laura do next?

After the reading, children's minds are further engaged by being asked to retell the story; put on a play about the story; tell the story with a flannel board; or draw, paint, or construct something about the story.

Retelling a story can be formal or informal. Informally, teachers ask children to talk about the story, asking what happened first, then what happened. Or the retelling could be more formal, with children taking turns retelling specific parts of the story.

Children could walk through a familiar story that involves a walk. You might draw a path with chalk on a sidewalk, or even the classroom floor. Children take turns playing Goldilocks and the three bears as they walk the path to the house. Other story paths children could walk are the path Little Red Riding Hood took, the path the wolf took to the houses of the three pigs, the path the Gingerbread Boy ran and so on. As children walk through the story, teachers may have to narrate, telling children in the beginning Goldilocks walked alone, then . . . , and so on.

Help children retell a story using purchased puppets or puppets they've made, a flannel board with cutout story characters, or story cards. Using discarded children's books, cut out and mount story characters and pictures of the setting, on tagboard cards. Children then use the picture cards to retell the story.

The visual arts offer children other ways to construct knowledge of story structure. Just using markers, crayons, and paper, children can recreate stories in any number of ways. Portraits, puppets, or drawings can be created of favorite characters, and murals and paintings made of a story's setting. Another activity is to fold a piece of construction paper into thirds for children to recreate a story's beginning, middle, and ending.

By engaging children in read-alouds through questions, discussions, and acting out or reflecting on stories, children will be using higher order thought processes. The focus on higher level questions, as well as an emphasis on applying word-recognition strategies, seem to provide children with the type of scaffolding necessary to become independent readers (Dolezal, Welsh, & Pressley, 2003). (See Figure 8.7 for an additional strategy to encourage independent reading.)

WRITING: DEVELOPING HABITS OF WRITING FOR A PURPOSE

Learning concepts of print and writing go hand in hand with language learning. The fourth set of standards revolve around children *developing the mechanics of writing and learning to write for a purpose.*

The language experience approach, which helps children make the letter, word, and sound connections, also gives them the idea of writing, and writing for a purpose. Still, children need to gain the skills involved in learning letter names and how to form them and to develop the skills of expressing themselves through their writing.

Figure 8.7. Books Around the Room

To encourage children to choose books for a variety of purposes,

- Keep a box of books on building near the block area
- Place books of nursery rhymes and songs in the housekeeping area so children can read to a baby who can't sleep
- Place science books, or books about fish or worms near the aquarium
- Make certain the classroom offers a balance of factual and fantasy books, biographies, poetry books, alphabet books, and other types of books for children's use

---

Learning Letter Names

Knowing letter names seems to be an important predictor of children's success in learning to read (Durrell, 1963). Letter knowledge is not the only skill children need to learn to read, however. Knowledge of letter names is probably related to concepts of print, as well as a sign of general intelligence, and a background of language and print-rich experiences is related to readiness to read (Vacca & Vacca, 2003)

Knowledge of letter names emerges from children's experiences in their home and school. The more print children see, the more letters adults point out to children, the more books are read to children, the more children see adults writing, the greater their knowledge of letter names. In good schools for young children letters are learned informally through ongoing activities.

Using children's names. What's most familiar to children? Meaningful? Their names. Teachers can use children's names to teach the letter names:

- List and display children's names often. Make a list of Our Halloween Parade, Who Are Going to the Apple Orchard. Make books of children's names with their photographs or a display of children's photos and their names.
- Point out and name the letters in children's names.
- For children just learning English, print their names in both their home language and English, Margarita —Margaret.
- Make two or more sets of name cards of stiff paper for children to use in the writing, library, or game area. No directions are necessary. Children will sort

through the stacks of names picking out those they know, those that are alike, or those of boys or girls.

Reading and making alphabet books. Alphabet books are another useful resource to use in helping children learn letter names. Teachers can read alphabet books to children. Alphabet books should include familiar objects and the names of these objects. Alphabet books about things unfamiliar to children such as *X* is for xenosaur, *A* is for aardvark, or *Z* is for zoril, are probably not as useful as alphabet books using familiar objects.

Teachers can have the children make class or individual alphabet books. One class made their own alphabet book following the scheme of *A, You're Adorable* (Kaye, 1998). In this book *A* is for adorable, *B* is for beautiful, *C* is for cutie, and so on. In another class the children made their own alphabet book using "love" words in both Spanish and English. Another classroom made an alphabet book of verbs. *A* was for arriving at school, *B* for bouncing balls, *Z* for zipping.

Teachers can make available wooden or plastic letters, rubber *a-b-c* stamps, and keyboards. Children can use these as models for writing their names, to sort and play with, or to assemble into sentences. Children can be encouraged to play Fish with the letters of the alphabet and make and play bingo games using letters of the alphabet.

Writing Emerges

Learning to write has its beginnings in children's scribbling and drawing. The random scribbles of childhood are golden. Scribbling is the very foundation on which children's writing emerges. From random, purely sensorimotor scribbles, controlled scribbles emerge. Children repeat circles and lines and begin to name parts of the scribble. Controlled scribbling begins anywhere between the ages of 3 and 6.

Some of the controlled scribbles are characterized as scribble writing. Scribble lines are completed as "letters to my grandma," "this says the story of the bears," or "here is my list." As early as 3 years of age children will distinguish their scribbles as drawings or writing. Three-year-old Alonso, whose father was a jockey, was asked to draw a picture of his father. He took the marker and drew a scribble that began at one end of the paper and went to the other, saying, "My daddy rides fast, faster, faster." When asked to write his daddy's name, he tightly gripped the marker and wrote a finer, tight line of letterlike forms.

Wordlike forms appear in children's scribbles. Usually these start as name scribbles as children try to write their names. The name may appear as one or two letters, or just letterlike forms that they call "My name, Joshua."

Other wordlike forms appear, and children begin to invent their own spelling of words. By inventing their own spelling children are mastering letter-sound correspondence, which helps prepare them for reading. When children write NIT for night, they are demonstrating that they know the sounds of the letters n/i/t. Later in their schooling, they'll learn, "Oh, no. *Night* isn't spelled *nit*, it's has a *ght*."

Invented spelling is important because when children invent their own spelling, they are asking themselves the following questions about letters, words, and sounds:

What does this word sound like?
What letters make that sound?
How do I write those letters?
What does the word mean?

Invented spelling follows definable, developmental stages (Bear & Templeton, 1998; Clay, 1979):

1. *Prephonemic spelling.* Children who know some letters begin to incorporate them into their drawings and paintings. They start by using one-to-one correspondence between beginning and ending consonants. Thus, prephonemic spelling might be "ct," for *cat*, because children hear and know the beginning and ending letters in the word *cat*. Or they may use "bt" for *boat*, or "dr" for *dear* when writing a letter to a friend. There is a one-to-one match between initial consonant and ending consonant.
2. *Phonemic spelling.* Around 6 or 7 years of age children incorporate vowels into their spelling of words. Now the word *boat* is written "bot" and the word *dear* may be written as "der." There still is a tendency to use one-to-one correspondence but this correspondence is more refined and logical substitutions are made for short vowels.
3. *Transitional spelling.* Transitional spelling includes chunks and patterns of letters that represent words. Knowing the rime *an*, children can write *can, pan, fan*, and so on. Or they use *ike* to spell *like, bike*, and *pike*. Children actively search for a match between the spoken word and letters.
4. *Conventional spelling.* By third grade most children have developed conventional spelling.

See Figure 8.8 for strategies for assessing children's phonemic awareness as indicated by their spelling.

Teachers can support children's emerging efforts at writing by encouraging classmates to write to each other. Set up a shoe box mail area. Boxes are labeled with children's names so children can place messages in each other's mailboxes. Or use a plastic shoe hanger with the slots labeled with children's names. Help children recognize other purposes for writing:

Figure 8.8. Assessing Phonemic Awareness

Children reveal their knowledge of phonemes in their invented spelling. When children write "th" for *the*, they have knowledge of the blend /th/. Or they may write "cr" for the word *car*, demonstrating that they know the beginning and ending sounds of the word. To assess specific task performance, ask children to:

- *Write their name.* Count the number of letter approximations, and the number of letters written correctly. Collect over time and record children's progress in writing their name conventionally.
- *Write a sentence you dictate.* For example, ask them to write, "The bus is coming." Analyze the number of letter sounds children approximate and write correctly. Repeat, collect sample writing, and chart children's progress.

- To express their ideas of an experience, or to tell how they felt about some event.
- To tell a story either fact or fantasy. They can create short stories about their own experiences or pretend stories.
- To tell how they did something.
- To explain what they found when studying something, such as worms.
- To make a book. Providing blank books (a couple of sheets of paper stapled together) encourages children to write books.

By having children read their own writing to each other, children will develop the idea that they gain meaning through their writing. Children could read their stories or books to the class, to a partner, to the school staff, and to their families.

IN SUMMARY

- Achievement of the language and literacy standards demand an integrated, language-rich environment in which children learn language as naturally as they live.
- Establishing the print-sound correspondence begins with children learning to listen attentively, to distinguish between environment sounds, to listen to and make music.
- Developing phonemic awareness goes hand in hand with learning to listen. At the same time children recognize environmental sounds, they are learning phonemes. Gaining phonemic awareness involves developing the skills of recognition of rhymes, seg-

A writing center fosters writing.

menting beginning and ending sounds in words, segmenting word parts, and being able to blend sounds.
- The language experience approach has the potential to fulfill every language and literacy standard. Because the LEA demands an experience, the approach makes print meaningful.
- Bringing meaning to the printed word is also fostered through interaction with books. Dialogical reading, including focus on story structure, introduces children to vocabulary new to them and helps children understand the meaning of the printed word.
- Learning concepts of print and writing go hand in hand with language learning. Children gain the skills involved in learning the names of letters and how to form them, and develop the skills of expressing themselves through their writing, inventing spelling as they go.

SAMPLE INVESTIGATION: CHILDREN STUDY THEIR PLAY YARD

Language and Literacy

Children of all ages will learn to observe their play yard and increase their vocabulary. They do so by learn-ing the names of the play yard equipment and categorizing equipment by function.

Activities

Selected standards

Practice listening and speaking skills.
Develop vocabulary, including naming objects (nouns) and motions (verbs).
Engage in drawing and writing activities.

The following experiences, which are designed to foster children's observation and vocabulary, are grouped by age. Based on their knowledge of the children they teach, teachers might begin slowly with those developed for toddlers. If, however, the children have already developed these skills, teachers might begin with the activities developed for older children.

Toddlers (*two–three years old*). With toddlers it's necessary to seize the teachable moment to name items on the play yard. One teacher, helping a toddler climb the steps of the slide, said, "Step up one stair, step up another. Now look, you're at the top of the slide. I'll stand at the bottom and catch you." She repeated the words *up* and *down*, *top* and *bottom*, as the child practiced her newfound skills. Here are other suggestions:

- *Ask questions*. When children seem lost and are just wandering about, focus their attention on specific pieces of play equipment. "Let's try the swing, you pump and I'll push." Or "Claire and Molly are playing in the sandbox, let's join them."
- *Compare and contrast responses*. Back in the classroom ask children to talk a bit about what they did outside. Ask them what they liked best and list their responses. Count the number of children who like the swing, slide, or other item the best. Begin comparing and contrasting different equipment. Ask children why they like different equipment. As they respond, compare and contrast different equipment and choices. "Tonja likes the swing best because she can 'fly to the sky.' Donald likes the slide because it has steps."
- *Repeat*. Continue to name items of equipment on the play yard until all children are able to talk about their favorite play yard item and why they like it.

Preschoolers (*three–four years old*). Most preschoolers will be familiar with the names of play yard equipment and able to begin to represent their ideas through drawings.

- *Provide children with clipboards and markers*. Ask them to use the clipboards to sketch what they see on the play yard.

- *Have children observe each other using the equipment.* Ask, "Where does Shawna put her hands?" "Look how Roberto uses his feet to balance." Use vocabulary to describe children's movements, "Slow, fast, quick." Ask children to talk about how they and other children move on different equipment and to sketch one another using equipment.
- *Discuss children's drawings.* Even though some of the drawings will be more like scribbles, children have definite ideas about what they observe. Taking children's work seriously, ask them to discuss their drawings. You could label the drawings, writing the words children use as they describe their drawings. "This is the shed." "This is the Billy Goats Gruff bridge," and so on.
- *Ask children to talk about their drawings to the total group.* This provides children with the opportunity to use vocabulary new to them and to see and listen to the ideas of others.
- *Create a display using children's drawings.* Entitle the display Our Play Yard. Write an explanation of the study so parents and other adults in the school will understand the purpose of the study and what children do.

Kindergarten children (four–five years old)

- Read books about play yards and playing out of doors. You might find books such as *The Playground* (Bailey & Huszar, 1998), *Miffy at the Playground* (Bruna, 1996), or *Let's Try It Out on the Playground* (Simon, Fauteux, & Cushman, 2005).

Experiences give children something to talk and write about.

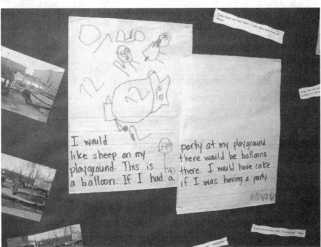

- After reading the book, ask children to document their learning by writing their own stories about their play yard. They might write stories about which pieces of equipment they like the best, what they can do on the play yard, or make a wish book of equipment they would like to have on their play yard.
- Make copies of the books to send home to children's families. Keep copies in the library area so children can enjoy one another's books.

Assessing Children's Learning

Observe

- Note how children are moving from incomplete to more complete sentences as they talk about their experiences on the play yard.
- Notice whether individual children are able to express their preferences of what to do when playing outside.
- Record when and how children name equipment and things on the play yard.
- Note children's use of verbs to describe their actions and the actions of others.
- Listen to children discuss their drawings of the play yard in front of the total group. Note how individuals becoming more articulate and able to express themselves in front of a group.
- Note how children respond to stories. Are they attentive? Record questions they ask, predictions made, and how they relate the story to their own experiences.

Interview

- Ask individual children to tell what they like best about their play yard, and what they like to do. Note and record nouns and verbs used.

Analyze samples of work

- Examine stories children write about their experiences on the play yard. Note when and how children use story structure including beginnings, middles, and endings. Note and record when and how children develop characters and describe a setting for their stories.
- Note and record how children respond to the stories of others, asking questions, relating the stories of others to their stories.
- Note, record, and analyze any invented spelling used by children. Count the number of correct letters used, correct syllabication, and use of conventional spelling.

CHAPTER 9

Integrating the Mathematics Standards

Naturally curious and eager to learn, children enter early educational programs with a great deal of mathematical knowledge. Researchers suggest that mathematic concepts begin early in life, perhaps during infancy. It seems as if children enter the world prepared to notice number as a feature of their environment (NRC, 2001a).

Much of their mathematical knowledge children learn through daily interactions with counting. Toddlers know when another has more trucks than they have, and they know when they have the biggest cookie.

The knowledge children gain naturally as they live is informal knowledge. In a preschool setting teachers build on children's informal knowledge and interest in mathematical ideas. Copley (2000) writes that the role of the teacher is to "provide a bridge between the child's informal knowledge of mathematics and the more formal school mathematics" (p. 47). With a focus on doing—actually experiencing concepts of numbers and mathematical skills through play and interaction with others—children's mathematical knowledge develops and grows into more formal ways of mathematical thinking (Baroody & Wilkins, 1999; CTB/McCraw-Hill, 2002).

As with the sciences, the arts, and other content areas, problem solving is key to the mathematics standards. "Problem solving should be the central focus of the mathematics curriculum. As such, it is a primary goal of all mathematics instruction and an integral part of all mathematical activity" (NCTM, 1989, p. 23).

The goals of this chapter are to

- Present the mathematics standards.
- Illustrate how to arrange an environment supportive of mathematical problem solving.
- Demonstrate how concepts of number and number operations, geometry and spatial awareness, measurement, patterns and relationships, and data organization are fully integrated into the total curriculum.

THE MATHEMATICS STANDARDS

The mathematics standards that follow should be considered as examples of those that may be presented to teachers. I derived these standards from two publications of the National Council of Teachers of Mathematics, *Curriculum and Evaluation Standards for School Mathematics* (1989) and *Principles and Standards for School Mathematics* (2000).

For the purposes of this book six standards were selected. The mathematics standards are both declarative, identifying content children are to learn, and procedural, identifying the mathematical problem-solving processes children are to gain.

1. Problem solving. Children will:
   1.a. Identify a problem
   1.b. Plan to solve it
   1.c. Execute the plan
   1.d. Reach a solution and reflect on it
2. Number and operations. Children will:
   2.a. Count with understanding
   2.b. Understand number operations, including adding and subtracting
3. Geometry and spatial awareness. Children will:
   3.a. Recognize and compare two- and three-dimensional shapes.
   3.b. Understand spatial relationships and use spatial reasoning
4. Measurement. Children will:
   4.a. Recognize that objects can be measured and compared by length, area, volume, weight, and time
   4.b. Compare and order objects according to these attributes
5. Patterns and relationships. Children will:
   5.a. Recognize and describe patterns
   5.b. Create patterns

6. Data description, organization, representation, and analysis. Children will:
   6.a. Construct graphs using objects.
   6.b. Create pictorial graphs.
   6.c. Use graphs to answer questions.

ARRANGING THE MATHEMATICAL PROBLEM-SOLVING ENVIRONMENT

An early childhood program that emphasizes *problem solving* will provide an environment that enables children to achieve the first set of math standards. Through an environment that fosters mathematical thinking and problem solving, children will be able to

- Use problem-solving approaches to investigate and understand mathematical content
- Identify appropriate problems from everyday life and mathematical situations
- Plan and apply strategies to solve a wide variety of problems
- Verify and interpret results with respect to the original problem
- Acquire confidence in using mathematics meaningfully

If children are to become mathematical problem solvers, they must have problems to solve. "Problem solving is not a distinct topic but a process that should permeate the entire program and provide the context in which concepts and skills can be learned" (NCTM, 1989, p. 23). Providing for problem solving through a mathematics-rich environment is one way to ensure that children will have opportunities to gain mathematics skills and concepts. In such an environment all kinds and types of materials are provided for children to work with. The materials are open-ended. There is no one right or wrong way to use the materials, nor is the goal for use of the materials predetermined. Limited or no directions are given for how to use the materials.

It is up to the child to determine not only which materials to use, but what to do with them, and whom to work with. Children are the ones who have to do the problem solving. They are the ones who have to set goals, make plans to achieve these, monitor their progress toward goal achievement, determine when their problem has been solved. Finally, children are the ones who receive the joys and rewards of setting goals and solving problems (see Figure 9.1).

The Physical Environment

As many early childhood teachers recognize, classrooms arranged around centers of interest are efficient

Figure 9.1. Stimulating Mathematical Problem Solving with Materials

A wide variety of materials give children the opportunity to

- *Recognize a problem:* "How can I make a fire truck with these materials?"
- *Make a plan to solve the problem:* "I'll need a box, some wheels, and a hose."
- *Monitor their progress in solving a problem:* "I have one pie pan for one wheel, now I need three more."
- *Reflect and think about the problem:* "I used red paper for the truck, next time I could paint it."

and effective ways of organizing the physical environment. Such classrooms reflect the idea that children learn through physical, mental, and social activity, not sitting still and listening to a teacher talk. When arranging centers of interest, teachers make certain that each center includes opportunities for mathematical thinking and problem solving.

Sociodramatic play center. Sociodramatic play areas are places where children can take on the role of others. Most often the sociodramatic play area will be a house where children take on the roles of mother, father, grandmother, baby, or some other family member. To provide children with plenty of opportunities to engage in mathematical thinking, the housekeeping area is equipped with the following materials:

- Measuring cups and spoons
- Small dishes and pots and pans to sort by shape, size, or use
- Hand-held calculators
- Blank calendars and markers
- Computers
- Wallets and purses with play money, void credit cards, and void checkbooks
- Shopping receipts
- Scales
- Counting books to read to the baby
- Greeting cards to sort by type (get well, birthday, Halloween, Valentines)

Other sociodramatic play areas are arranged from time to time. A visit to a grocery store, plant nursery, veterinarian's office, or the school office could lead to setting up a place where children can act out the roles of clerk and shopper, vet and worried pet owner, and so on. These centers would include cash registers, cash receipts, play money, office equipment, things to count, rubber number stamps, and calendars.

Visual and musical arts centers. The visual arts offer children many opportunities to experience mathematical ideas. Children can

- Measure and mix paints, clay, or playdough
- Create patterns with art materials
- Measure papers and materials with arbitrary measuring sticks or rulers
- Use a variety of shapes to create collages
- Solve mathematical problems as they construct objects from boxes or other pieces of scrap materials
- Sort, categorize, and count all kinds of different textured papers—tissue paper, watercolor, construction, shiny, smooth, or rough

The music area, equipped with a variety of rhythm instruments, allows children to create musical patterns. Including music books so children can see and count notes and lines, is another way of fostering children's mathematics skills. The music center might include

- A box of several kinds of bells—small bells, cow bells, decorative bells, sleigh bells, and other bells—for children to classify according to the sounds the bells make and their size
- A set of different-size drums to sort and classify by type and loudness of sounds that can be produced
- Tape recorders for children to record and listen to counting songs, chants, and rhymes

Language learning center. The book area should include repetitive books that involve children in counting, recognizing number, and using number operations. These might include

- Catalogs to use as "wish books" or to categorize items, for example, as toys or clothes; things I want or do not want; and so on
- Counting and other books with mathematical ideas
- Flannel boards with cutout numbers to use in acting out books of counting rhymes or chants
- Books that link math with ongoing projects, such as books about stores or supermarkets predominately displayed after a trip to a supermarket or store
- A lending library of number books for children to check out and take home with them
- Class or individual written books that include mathematical ideas

Manipulatives center. This center, sometimes called the mathematics center, is equipped with

- Things for children to count—boxes of shells, large buttons
- Large seeds, beans, beads (all too large to be stuffed into noses or ears)
- Balance scales and objects to weigh, such as acorns, rocks, nuts, bolts, and screws (too large to stuff anywhere)
- Sorting trays, boxes, or cloths divided into sections give children the idea of sorting
- Commercial items, such as plastic or wooden farm animals, birds, zoo animals, toys, trains, small dolls, trucks, and so on, to sort, weigh, and count
- A collection of wooden dolls of various lengths and diameters to sort and seriate
- Unit cubes and blocks, including some patterns
- Beads and strings to create patterns, sometimes with patterns to follow
- Clipboards, paper, and markers to record findings
- Plastic and wooden numbers, rubber number stamps, paper and markers so children can write numbers
- A deck of cards to sort or play Concentration or other games
- Games such as matching games, lotto, dominoes, and counting; Bingo for older children
- Clock and number puzzles that relate directly to mathematics, simple puzzles with shapes divided into fractions
- Other puzzles for children to build spatial awareness and awareness of shapes
- Geoboards and rubber bands

Block center. Blocks are the most important tool for mathematical learning. Through play with blocks children come in contact with the following concepts:

- Number
- Number operations
- Weight and height
- Balance
- Symmetry

Equip the block area with unit blocks, including specialized forms (arches, curves), large hollow blocks, plastic blocks, various types of interlocking blocks, wooden animals, and people.

Science center. Math and science are natural allies (Seefeldt & Galper, 2004). Science centers offer children opportunities to observe, classify, compare, measure, experiment, make predictions, and reach conclusions that are communicated to others. In the science area children might find:

- Scales of all types with objects to weigh and forms to fill in so children can record the heaviest, smallest, and so on

Mathematical problem solving requires open ended materials.

- Tape and other measures so children can measure acorns, worms, or other objects and things
- Machines to take apart or use—clocks, pencil sharpeners, instrument-panel boards (which have been safety proofed)
- Sand and water—for children to gain math concepts through the use of a variety of containers from which to pour and measure sand and water, to observe conservation of water and sand, determine properties of water and sand, count the number of cups of water a bucket holds, and so on.

Woodworking center. Here children find wood and woodworking tools. Children receive instruction and practice in the safe use of saws, screw drivers and screws, hammer and nails. Measuring tools are a part of the woodworking area. Children explore, with the supervision of an adult, the properties of wood and how to join pieces. Then they might design a plan or pattern, select pieces of wood, and measure and join the wood to create the object they designed.

Computer/technology center. The computer area would include mathematics software for children to

practice math concepts. Children can type and manipulate numbers using the computer. Hand-held calculators, along with markers and paper to record findings, are also a part of this area.

The Social Environment

All the materials in the world and all the time to explore, measure, weigh, and play with the materials cannot give children the problem-solving skills required to fulfill the mathematics standards without the guidance of adults. The role of the teacher is to

- Deliberately use the language of mathematics in connection with children's explorations and activities
- Deliberately focus children's experiences with materials on mathematical ideas
- Make certain that all children—boys and girls, children with and without disabilities, and children of

Joint activities, counting the days until eggs hatch, involve children in mathematics.

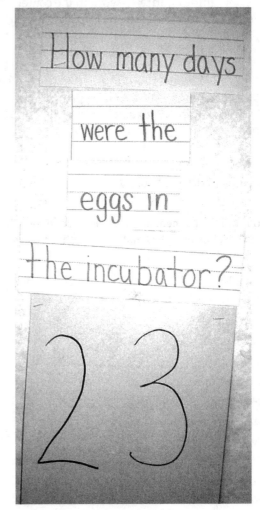

all racial and ethnic groups—are fully involved in all facets of mathematics
- Use center time to observe children's use of math vocabulary and ideas, and record these observations for planning future math activities

Deliberate use of vocabulary. As children are working with objects and materials, teachers can use math vocabulary (see Figure 9.2). Connecting children's actions to words, teachers can say, "Take just half a sandwich." "Here is a quarter of an apple." "The window is a rectangle." "The yield sign is a triangle" (Seefeldt & Wasik, 2002).

Entering into conversations with children about what they are doing gives teachers an understanding of individual children's knowledge of math. Teachers can note the words children use and how they handle math ideas. With this knowledge, teachers can add materials that will allow children to practice existing math skills. Other materials will be added to nudge children's thinking into areas of mathematics new to them.

A focus on mathematical concepts. Teachers observe and guide children's work in the centers. They deliberately introduce math concepts into children's experiences, and deliberately expand and extend children's existing math ideas. Teachers carefully structure their interactions to match what children already know with what they want them to learn. Vygotsky (1986) called this teaching in the "zone of proximal development"; Bredekamp (1998) said it was teaching on the edge of what children already know.

Figure 9.2. Math Vocabulary

To fulfill the mathematics standards, children will need to develop an understanding of math words and phrases, such as

More, less

Most, least

Large, small

Smaller than

Larger than

Different than

If—then

Same, different

Quarter, half, whole

Rectangle, square, circle, triangle

Straight, angle

By entering into joint activities with children and working collaboratively with them on a problem or task, such as comparing the size of seeds from different plants, teachers encourage children to use math. "How many seeds do you have?" asks a teacher. "Let's count them." "Which is the largest seed? The smallest?" are questions that can be asked without interrupting children's free explorations and experimentation with seeds.

Taking care not to disrupt the flow of children's play, teachers can comment on math concepts. Teachers might say to a child lugging a suitcase out of the housekeeping play area, "That suitcase must be heavy!" Or to the child rocking a baby doll, "How old is your baby? How much does she weigh?"

Teachers can challenge children's math ideas by saying:

- Tell me about your pattern.
- What part of your pattern is repeated?
- Your pattern uses the same color blocks. Tell me about it.
- Tell me which side of the sorting tray has more.
- Which group of blocks weighs more?
- Which book has the most pages?
- What does this graph mean?

Teachers act as models for children. They can make sure children observe them as they take attendance, counting the children that are present and those that are not. Children observe teachers counting snacks and permission slips, or measuring food for the hamsters.

Teachers also model problem-solving behaviors. "Let's try it this way." Or "I wonder what would happen if we. . . ." And they assist children trying to solve a problem. "Here, I'll hold the tape measure while you pull it to the other end of the table" (Seefeldt & Galper, 2000).

Inclusion of all children. All children—boys and girls, those with special needs, and those of differing racial and ethnic groups—have to be equally involved in mathematics activities. For children with special needs, first consider accessibility. How will the child with special needs be able to experience mathematical ideas and concepts? Can the child in a wheelchair negotiate the centers? Are the pathways adequate? Are tables low enough for the child? How will you provide mathematical experiences for the child who cannot hold or manipulate objects?

Make a special effort to encourage girls in math experiences such as block building or taking apart instrument panels or other machines. Historically, girls have tended to avoid math. Girls make up only a small percentage of students in computer science courses and take English courses in greater numbers than boys and fewer math courses. A larger proportion of boys than of girls receives top scores on the National Assessment of Education Progress (American Association of University Women [AAUW], 1998).

Researchers suggest that math avoidance begins early in children's lives (AAUW, 1998). Thus teachers of young children should make certain that girls are as involved in mathematics-rich centers as boys. Teachers can ask girls to chose to spend time in the block area or computer and technology areas, and deliberately involve them in mathematical problem solving and other math activities.

Observation and assessment of children's learning. Center time is prime time for observing individual children's skills and capabilities with mathematical ideas. Some teachers take three or four note cards with them during center time with children's names on the cards. Then they focus some part of the center time on observing just these three children, noting the math concepts they use and those they are just learning. These notes are then transferred to a computer file for the individual child. The file is then used to assess children's knowledge in the different mathematical content areas.

The observations are also used to identify the general level of mathematical knowledge of the entire group. With this knowledge teachers can select materials to add to or remove from centers of interest. Those that no longer challenge children's math ideas are removed and replaced with more sophisticated materials.

CONCEPTS OF NUMBER AND OPERATIONS

Concepts of *counting and number operations*, the second set of math standards, begin early. During the period of infancy and toddlerhood, children begin developing mathematical skills, concepts as well as misconceptions of number (NRC, 2001a). Three-year-olds say, "He's got more than me." They know they are 3 years old; "I'm this many," said Belinda, holding up three fingers. Children sing number songs, Five Little Chickadees, and Ten in the Bed. And children, even as young as 3, count to ten.

But counting is a complex process. One that involves thinking. To count, children must be able to think about what is being counted and what things are not counted; then they have to pair the item they are counting with the number name. Finally, children have to understand that the number they say last represents the number of objects they have counted (NRC, 2001a).

Children under age 5 generally do not have an idea of quantity. Just being able to say number names does not mean children have a sense of number. The 3- or

Concepts of number develop gradually.

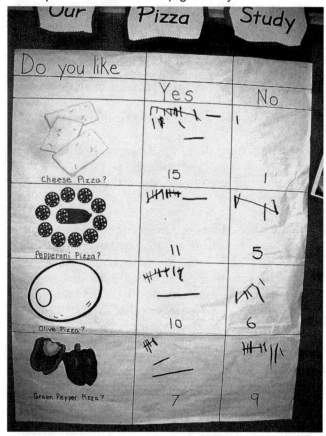

4-year-old who can say number names in correct sequence from 1 to 20, or even from 1 to 100, may know the names of numbers but not have a sense of number. Even though they can name the numbers, they are unable to tell you what number comes before or after another. Nor can children generally match the numbers they are saying with the objects the numbers represent (Copley, 2000). This is one-to-one correspondence. These young children are likely to count six cookies on a plate saying, "One, two, five, seven," or five buttons on their coat as "One, three, four, six."

Around 4 or 5 years of age children are able to count rationally and use this skill in solving problems. This means that now children with five buttons on their coat will count the buttons, "One, two, three, four, five," and know that the word *five* represents the number of buttons on their coat. This is because now children have a mental structure of number and have assimilated number words into this structure.

Four- and five-year-olds will be able to tell you how many more cookies they need for each child to have two, how many blocks are needed to complete a building, or who has the most markers. They are able to tell you, "I had three books, but I gave one to my sister; now I have two."

Counting is a complex process. It involves:

- Learning the vocabulary of mathematics including number names
- Understanding one-to-one correspondence
- Understanding cardinality: that the last word said when counting a group of objects, such as 4, represents 4 objects
- Saying number words in a consistent, reproducible order
- Understanding that things can be counted in any sequence without changing the results
- Experiencing the number operations of adding and subtracting

How do children learn to count? By counting. Number sense evolves from the total classroom experience (NCTM, 1991). Children expand their understanding of number by performing operations with numbers. Children will compare numbers, classify, and do simple adding and taking away operations (NCTM, 2000; NCTM/NAEYC, 2002). In good schools for young children counting is integrated into the total day. Children can

- Count the number of children who can work in the woodworking area
- Give each child a cup and napkin
- Decided what they will do first, then second, during work time
- Tell how many more children can sit at the table with them
- Count the number of blocks in their building
- Count the number of block arches they'll need
- Count the number of cups of sand it takes to fill another container
- Count the number of cups of water and flour to make bread
- Tell how many fish are in the aquarium and how many there will be when two new fish are added
- Count the number of children who are not in school

In addition to functional counting—counting with a real purpose throughout the day—children need to experience more intentional and explicit counting experiences. These might include playing board games that involve counting, other counting games, or the activities in the "Sample Investigation" at the end of the chapter. (See Figure 9.3 for assessment of children's counting.)

GEOMETRY AND SPATIAL AWARENESS

Knowledge of *geometry and spatial awareness*, the third set of math standards, begins early in life, as number sense does. Two- and three-year-olds recognize the

Figure 9.3. Assessing Children's Counting

Place 10 objects on a table.

- Ask children, individually, to count the beads, trucks, or plastic animals on the table. They can touch them if they wish. Record when the child loses one-to-one correspondence. The last number in correct association gives an indication of the child's ability to use one-to-one correspondence.

- When the objects are arranged in sets of two, three, and five, ask the child which set contains the most, the least, and which set has more than another.

- When the objects are placed in a row, ask the child how many objects there are.

- Ask the child to hand you the first, second, and last object.

- Now place five objects in front of the child, and place the other objects to one side. With these five objects, ask the child to:

  a. Take away two and tell you how many are left.

  b. Add enough objects to make six.

difference between balls and blocks, and can put round and square pegs into their appropriate holes in a sorting board. Twos will draw scribble circles, with lines that go around and around. Three-year-olds can draw a circle stopping at one revolution. By 4 years of age children will draw shapes recognizable as squares and will tell you, "A square has four pointy corners." By age 6 or 7 children can draw triangles and describe the difference between squares and rectangles.

Young children's spatial awareness of themselves in relation to people and objects in space, appears to be more advanced than their numerical skills (NCTM, 2000). As young children climb up, in, and under objects in their environment, or experience themselves being lifted high into the air, or swinging and sliding, they are developing ideas of themselves in space. Through their activities they develop perceptual awareness of location, and two- and three-dimensional creations.

Since the time of Froebel, geometry has been a part of the early childhood curriculum. Recognizing that children's developing concepts of and space begin early in life, Froebel introduced balls, blocks, spheres, and cubes as "gifts" in the kindergarten curriculum. Three-, four-, and five-year-old children were to play with these objects with the goal of understanding the concept of unity.

The goals of geometry and spatial awareness in today's good schools for young children are more refined and complex. The concepts children are to gain are the following:

- Geometric shapes are two- and three-dimensional.
- Two- and three-dimensional geometric shapes have characteristics and properties that can be analyzed.
- Investigations and predictions can be made about geometric shapes.
- Children's spatial sense is their awareness of themselves in relation to people and objects around them in space.
- Spatial visualization and reasoning can be used to solve problems.
- Geometry describes and classifies the physical world we live in.

To help children develop concepts of geometry, teachers can provide two- and three-dimensional materials for children to sort, group, and build or construct with, and explicitly draw children's attention to shapes around them. For instance, teaching children to play group circle games such as Duck, Duck, Goose, Ring Around the Rosy, Farmer in the Dell, Did you Ever See a Lassie, and so on, gives children physical and social experiences with circles. Teachers can point out that in order to play the game, children must form a circle. They may say, "Everyone hold another's hand, now holding hands, take two steps backward," and a circle is formed.

Other games, such as Simon Says, give children additional opportunities to experience themselves in space. Exploration of shapes and self in space can continue by making large shapes of masking tape on the floor. Children can walk around triangles, circles, squares, and rectangles. As they walk, teachers can ask them to see how many children can fit inside the square or the circle, or how many steps they have to take to walk around a circle or triangle.

Outdoor play offers children opportunities to study themselves in space and become familiar with shapes. Children can find shapes in the play yard equipment. The jungle gym may make squares, and the swing set, a large triangle. Inside the classroom ask children to draw items of equipment as they think about the shapes they saw. Or you could provide pieces of cutout shapes similar to those found in the play yard and have children make a collage of play yard equipment using the shapes. Have children tell what they were drawing or making and label their work. Display children's work with a mural. Entitle the mural "We Study Shapes on the Play Yard" and mount children's work on the mural.

Use of computer programs follows actual experiences with shapes and space. Programs allow children to move geometric objects along paths or in space. With Logo, children are able to learn about geometric shapes, not so much from their perception of objects as from the actions they perform on these objects. When children have themselves moved on paths, they can learn to think of a turtle's actions as ones they performed.

MEASUREMENT

As children classify, sort, compare, and order materials, they begin to use concepts of *measurement*, the fourth set of mathematic standards. When working with materials, children will need to find a block that fits their building, the largest bucket to fill, or which is heavier—an apple or a pear.

The National Council of Teachers of Mathematics (NCTM, 1989) suggests that children not use formal, conventional measurement tools such as rulers, yard sticks, or thermometers until well into the second grade. Before children can understand formal measurement, they need to develop the understanding that the length or weight of an object remains the same regardless of whether its position is changed. This involves the idea that measurement can be expressed as a multiple of any number of units.

"How long does this need to be?"

Just because children are not able to understand formal measurement, however, does not mean they should not use measurement. The NCTM (1989) recommends that children measure their world using arbitrary measures—their hands, feet, a piece of rope, balance scales, and containers to fill and spill.

The goals for measurement activities are that children will

- Begin to find out which is heavier/lighter, taller/shorter, longer/shorter, big/bigger, less/more, hot/cold, fast/slow, or which container holds less or more.
- Develop the vocabulary of measurement, using words such as *more* or *less* and so on.
- Use arbitrary measures, such as a piece of string, to solve problems as they play, construct, build, or create objects.
- Begin to recognize the need for standard units of measurement.

Measuring activities are integrated throughout the entire curriculum. Outside children might walk the play yard to find out how many footsteps it takes to walk one side, or if children are older, the entire perimeter. Count with children as they reach higher numbers and help them record their finding. Remember, however, that this activity is designed to introduce children to the idea of measuring, not to teach accurate measurement. Keep the activity informal so every child who wants to can walk the perimeters.

There are other things children can measure on the play yard. Provide them with a stopwatch or old alarm clock. Show them how to measure

- Time spent on a piece of equipment
- How fast they can run across the yard
- How far they can jump on one foot, on two feet

"How much do you add?"

Or have them measure the time one child spends on a piece of equipment. This is especially useful if you have a new or very attractive piece of equipment that everyone wants to use at once. Ask children how long each child's turn should be. Step in if they overestimate time, adjusting the time to 2 minutes or 50 seconds or some other reasonable limit. You might provide a clipboard and marker so children can sign up for their turn.

PATTERNS AND RELATIONSHIPS

Basic to mathematical insight is the ability to recognize *patterns and relationships*, the fifth group of math standards. The ability to see and create patterns supports children in learning to see relationships, to find connections, and to make generalizations and predictions. "Understanding patterns nurtures the kind of mathematical thinking that helps children become problem solvers and abstract thinkers. It is a problem solving tool" (NCTM, 1998). Knowledge of patterns implies that children are developing ideas of predictability and repetition. They are able to

- Sort and order objects on the basis of some characteristic
- Recognize patterns in their environment
- Create patterns
- Remember a pattern that uses numbers

"I know," said a child whose parents had recently divorced and had joint custody. "It's like a pattern. On Monday, Wednesday, and Friday nights I go to my daddy's house. On Tuesday, Thursday, and Sunday I go to my mommy's house." Patterns are indeed everywhere. All you need to do is draw children's attention to patterns that already exist.

Children may have patterns on their sweaters or other clothing. There may be patterns of tiles throughout the school. The very rhythm of life is a pattern. We get up, go to school, come home. Day follows night, and spring follows winter. Repetitive stories, chants and poems have patterns. "Ten in the Bed," "Shoo Fly," "Five Little Speckled Frogs" and so on have rhymes that repeat and repeat.

To gain the skills of the standards, children will need to order and sort a variety of manipulatives. Placing long shoestrings next to the box of large wooden or other types of beads in the manipulatives area gives children the opportunity to make patterns. When they do create a pattern, such as alternating red and blue beads, comment on the color of their pattern. There really is no limit to the manipulatives that can be used to create patterns. The nuts and bolts in the sorting area could be sorted to create patterns. Unit blocks, bells, buttons, and any of the

Patterns are fun to create.

other manipulatives in the math or manipulatives center will be used by children to create patterns.

Provide children with patterns to copy. Patterns may come with boxes of plastic tiles, or you can create patterns for children to copy. Make patterns useful to children. If they are creating wall paper for the housekeeping area, show them how they can make a pattern with sponges. Older children can make wrapping paper by creating patterns with rubber stamps.

Keep in mind the mathematics involved in recognizing and making patterns (NCTM, 1991). You might ask, "What comes next?" as children are stringing beads, or "How are these patterns alike?" "How do they differ?" "Look, these patterns are the same but one is made with beads, the other with nuts and bolts." "Describe your pattern to the group." "Can you repeat the pattern with these seeds?" "Your pattern uses only red blocks, tell me about it."

DATA DESCRIPTION, ORGANIZATION, REPRESENTATION, AND ANALYSIS

Graphing is one way of *describing, organizing, representing, and analyzing data*, the final set of math stan-

dards. Through firsthand experiences children will learn to

- Construct and create a variety of graphs
- Use graphs to answer questions

Graphing is one way of communicating a great deal of information in an organized way. Learning to make and read graphs requires a great deal of abstract thought. Graphs give children a way of organizing information that allows them to ask and answer questions. The visual representation found in a graph gives children a new way to understand information and reach conclusions. By basing graphing on children's meaningful experiences and involving them in making and reading graphs, children gain initial ideas of graphing.

Start graphing with concrete objects. If you are studying which cereal is the group favorite, bring in single-serving boxes of a variety of cereals. Children select their favorite. Cereal boxes are stacked together by type, and the tallest stack represents the group's favorite cereal.

One 3-year-old group studied babies. The children tasted and ate baby cereal and the cereal they regularly ate and graphed their preference. The teacher made a graph with two columns. At the top of one column was a cutout picture of a box of the cereal children regularly ate, the other column had a picture of a jar of baby cereal. Children were to put a mark under the one they liked to eat. Of course, all of the children wrote their name (or made a mark) under the box of adult cereal. None marked the baby cereal. A visitor to the classroom asked a group of 3-year-olds who were looking at the graph, "What does this mean?" The children then told the entire story of having to taste baby cereal, which was

A graph communicates a great deal of information.

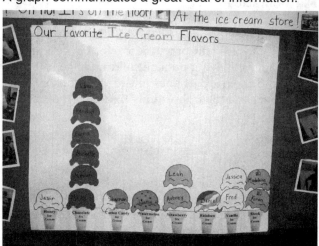

really awful, but they had a chance to make their views known by marking the graph. "And none of us liked the yucky baby cereal," the 3-year-olds explained, pointing to the graph.

Teachers may begin the graphing process using blocks with children's names on them to create bar graphs depicting how tall children are, which bus they ride to school, or how many vote for one thing or another. Graphs could be made of children's shoe sizes, birthdays, eye and hair color, ages, or favorite books. The idea is for children to be able to organize their ideas in ways that communicate to others.

IN SUMMARY

- Children need physical and social environments that promote mathematical problem-solving experiences.
- Concepts of number and operations begin early in life. The complex idea of counting is fostered by learning mathematical vocabulary and understanding one-to-one correspondence and cardinality.
- Geometry and spatial awareness develop in relation to people and objects in space. Children "do" geometry, acting on their environment, rather than memorizing rules of geometry.
- Measurement takes place as children classify, sort, compare and order materials. As they do so, they need to find a way to measure and record their findings.
- Understanding that there are predictable patterns and relationships is basic to mathematical thinking.

SAMPLE INVESTIGATION: CHILDREN STUDY THEIR PLAY YARD

Mathematics

While playing out of doors children have the opportunity to use and practice developing concepts of mathematics. Playing outside children have objects to count and measure, shapes and sizes to observe and categorize, and the opportunity to use the vocabulary of mathematics.

Selected standards

Develop concepts of counting
Compare objects by size
Make and use measurements in problem solving and
    everyday situations

Activities

Toddlers (two–three years old)

- Spontaneously count, while children are engaged in activities on the play yard. You can involve the children in counting the number waiting for their turn on a new piece of equipment, the number of steps they take to go up the slide, the number of bars they can hold onto as they traverse across the small jungle gym, or the number who can swing at the same time.

Preschoolers (four–five years old)

- One day focus on things that are big and little on the play yard. Ask the children to identify the largest or biggest piece of equipment on the yard. Then look around at trees and other plants or items on the play yard: Which is the biggest? Then switch and ask children to focus on the smallest things on the play yard. Suggest they look not only at equipment but really small things like grains of sand or blades of grass.
- Back in the classroom read *What is Big?* (Wing, 1969). Then make a class booklet called "The Biggest Thing

Let's count how many steps you can take.

I Know in the Play Yard." Children think of the biggest thing they know of and draw a picture of it. Remember that preschooler's drawings may be more in the form of scribbles than realistic drawings. Nevertheless, they can tell about what they were drawing and give it a title. Write what they say about their drawing on the bottom of the page along with their names. Compile the pages between two pieces of construction paper with the title and the author, such as by "Children in the Red Room."

- Repeat to focus on small. Reread *What is Big?* (Wing, 1969). Ask children to think of the smallest thing they found on the play yard. Suggest they think broadly and consider grains of sand, blades of grass, tiny insects, and so on. One child said that worm eggs were the smallest thing. She explained that the teacher always asked children to wash their hands after coming in from the play yard because there may be worm eggs on them. The teacher had said that they get on your hands when you play in the dirt and they are so tiny you can't even see them. Make another class booklet titled "The Smallest Thing I Know."

Kindergarten children (four–five years old)

- Count and categorize specific items on the play yard. For example, ask children to count all of the pieces of climbing equipment, the items in the sand and water tables, the number of bikes or other wheel toys, and so on. Reach conclusions about which type of equipment is most prevalent on the play yard.
- Another day have the children go outside to find the tallest and shortest pieces of equipment. Measure one of the children, and talk with the children about how to figure out how many children stacked head to toe it would take to equal the tallest piece of equipment on the yard.

- Introduce ideas of width and find the widest and narrowest pieces of equipment on the yard.
- Document children's work by using pictures, either photos or cutout catalog pictures of equipment, make a graph of the tallest and shortest, widest and narrowest pieces of equipment.

Assessing Children's Learning

Observe

- Notice children's use of number concepts as they play. Informally note and record how and what children count. Are they able to use number words? How sequential is their counting? Is there evidence of one-to-one correspondence?
- Record when children use number concepts to solve problems on the play yard.

Interview

- Ask individual children to count something on the play yard. Make note of evidence of one-to-one correspondence, or other counting and number concepts.
- Have children identify the largest things they know on the play yard—the smallest and tallest, the widest and narrowest.

Assign tasks to perform

- Ask children to hop, swing a given number of times, or climb a given number of steps. Note and record children's abilities to accurately follow directions.
- Using arbitrary measures, such as a length of yarn, ask children to measure how many times the yarn goes around a piece of play yard equipment.

CHAPTER 10

Integrating the Social Studies Standards

The social studies are comprised of a wide variety of subject matter disciplines, including anthropology, civic education, economics, history, geography, and sociology. To organize this vast amount of information, the National Council for the Social Studies (NCSS, 1994) has designated ten themes. These themes encompass content from many disciplines. The ten themes are:

I. *Culture.* The study of culture prepares students to answer questions such as: What are the common characteristics of different cultures? . . .

II. *Time, continuity, and change.* Humans seek to understand their historical roots and to locate themselves in time. . . .

III. *People, places, and environments.* The study of people, places, and human-environment interactions assists students as they create their spatial view and geographic perspectives of the world beyond their personal locations. . . .

IV. *Individual development and identity.* Personal identity is shaped by one's culture, by groups, and by institutional influences. . . .

V. *Individuals, groups, and institutions.* Institutions such as schools, churches, families, government agencies, and the courts play an integral role in people's lives. . . .

VI. *Power, authority, and governance.* Understanding the historical development of structures of power, authority, and governance and their evolving functions in contemporary U.S. society and other parts of the world is essential for developing civic competence. . . .

VII. *Production, distribution, and consumption.* Because people have wants that often exceed the resources available to them, a variety of ways have evolved to answer questions such as: What is to be produced? How are goods and services to be distributed? . . .

VIII. *Science, technology, and society.* Modern life as we know it would be impossible without technology and the science that supports it. . . .

IX. *Global connections.* The realities of global interdependence require understanding the increasingly important and diverse global connections among world societies. . . .

X. *Civic ideals and practices.* An understanding of civic ideals and practices of citizenship is critical to full participation in society. . . . (NCSS, 1994, "Executive Summary")

The goal of the social studies is as all encompassing as its subject matter. Although the goal of all education in a democracy is to prepare children to become productive members of society, the social studies are uniquely suited to achieving this goal. The National Council for the Social Studies (1994) believes that the primary purpose of the social sciences is to help young children develop the ability to make informed and reasoned decisions for the public good as citizens of a culturally diverse democratic society in an interdependent world.

Somehow, it seems inappropriate to include young children in the overwhelming social studies goal of preparing children to become citizens of a democratic world. But it is especially when children are young that social studies is a valued part of the curriculum. Research shows that it is during the early years of life that the foundation for all other learning is formed (NRC/IOM, 2000). During the period of early childhood, children learn who they are in relation to others and their environment.

Beginning right from the very start of life, children are exposed to and learn who they are from the culture they are born into. The culture teaches children about power, authority, and global connections. Through the use of the science and technology of the culture, children recognize the importance of creativity.

Infants learn time through the routines of the day. As they grow and change, and observe others grow and change, they become aware of the continuity of human life. Their role in economics, as producers and consumers, takes place daily. By participating in the life of their family and the small democracy of the classroom, children gain ideas of civic participation.

By focusing on the themes and standards of the social studies pertinent to young children, teachers can take children's informal experiences in their world and turn them into learning experiences (NCSS, 1994). Through the learning experiences in good schools for young children, children should gain the knowledge and skills embedded in the following social studies standards.

THE SOCIAL STUDIES STANDARDS

The social studies standards that follow should be considered as examples of those that may be presented to teachers. I derived these standards from those of the National Council for the Social Studies (NCSS, 1994), McREL's *Content Knowledge: A Compendium of Standards and Benchmarks for K–12 Education* (Kendall & Marzano, 2004), and the *Pre-K Standards* of CTB/ McGraw-Hill (2002). I also consulted the standards from the Geography Education Standards Project (GESP, 1994), the National Standards for History for Grades K–4 (NCHS, 1996), and the Center for Civic Education (CCE, 1994).

The social studies standards begin with kindergarten and extend through Grade 12. Further, there are an overwhelming number of standards that could be considered as a part of the social studies. Therefore, it was necessary to select the most salient standards for inclusion in this chapter and those that best pertain to children under the age of 7 or 8.

The social studies standards are both declarative and procedural in nature. They define content children should know, as well as what children should be able to do in selected social studies content areas.

1. Culture. Children will:
   1.a. Develop self-identity
   1.b. Develop knowledge and respect for others
   1.c. Develop knowledge of their culture and the culture of others
2. Time, continuity, and change. Children will:
   2.a. Develop a sense of time
   2.b. Gain ideas of change
   2.c. Develop an understanding of the continuity of life
3. People, places, and environment. Children will:
   3.a. Develop knowledge that the earth is the place they live
   3.b. Develop knowledge of different earth surfaces and forms
   3.c. Compare how they travel on the earth
   3.d. Become acquainted with maps and their use

4. Production, distribution, and consumption. Children will:
   4.a. Become aware of needs and wants
   4.b. Become producers and consumers
5. Civic ideals and practices. Children will:
   5.a. Care for themselves
   5.b. Give up some of their individuality for the good of the group
   5.c. Learn to vote and follow the will of the majority

SELF, OTHERS, AND CULTURE

The standards call for children to *develop self-identity, respect for others, and knowledge of their culture and the culture of others*. Before individuals can effectively relate to others, or care for or respect the views of others, they must first know and respect themselves. As children begin the lifelong process of developing self-identity, they also begin the process of learning to respect and relate to others.

Self-Identity

Developing self-identity and learning to relate to others are like two sides of the same coin. Within the family unit and community, children—from the moment of birth or even before—begin developing knowledge of their own self-worth, who they are, and what they can do. To know who they are, to feel valued and worthy, children must know that they are valued by others. In the early childhood setting this means that children's individuality is valued, respected, and protected (Pastnaik, 2003). In good schools for young children, all children

- Are called by their names.
- Have the opportunity to make choices and are encouraged to do so, so that they develop a sense of being in control of their own lives.
- Are protected—no child is permitted to bully, taunt, tease or harm another.
- Have an abundance of ways to learn a given skill or piece of information. For example, children could learn the characteristics of shapes by building with blocks, putting puzzles together, or making a collage.
- Have opportunities to express themselves creatively.
- Understand that thinking is not only accepted but respected.
- Recognize that they are valued members of the group. For example, they are given real responsibilities to complete and are included as participants in small- and large-group activities (see Figure 10.1).

Children who have a well-developed self-identity know that they are loved and respected; they know the

Figure 10.1. Developing Self-Identity Is Integral to the Entire Curriculum

---

Language Learning

Learning that each child has a name, and that other objects and events also have names

Number Concepts

Counting the number of children who can work at the woodworking table, or the number of children in class; learning the ages of the children

Life Sciences

Charting children's physical growth; learning about the need for water, nutrition, physical care and exercise

The Arts

Expressing emotions, ideas, and experiences through the visual, musical, and theatrical arts

---

names of the people who care for them, and they are able to make independent choices about what they will do. They confidently express their ideas, likes, and dislikes, and share their emotions, both verbally and through the arts. These children have moved from overly critical assessments of self to realistic judgments of themselves as worthy individuals.

Knowledge of and Respect for Others

Like developing self-identity, learning to relate to others is a lifelong process. Observing children of different ages at play reveals how children develop social skills and learn to relate to each other very gradually (Berk, 2001).

Infants, while enjoying being with other infants, engage in solitary play. Infants may even treat one another as play things or objects. In one child care center, 13-month-old Sonja noticed Kevin sipping water from a cup. Toddling over Sonja grabbed the cup from him and tried to drink from it. Unaware that Kevin had feelings or that the cup belonged to Kevin, Sonja was completely surprised at Kevin's loud, screaming protest.

Parallel play is enjoyed by toddlers who appear to be playing with one another, yet each is carrying out individual play. A group of three 2-year-olds were engaged in making sand cakes in the sand area. They appeared to be taking part in a joint effort. But when the teacher listened to them, he found that each child was playing quite alone. As one child patted the sand into

containers, she said, "One, two, three—one for me, one for mommy, one for daddy." Another was dumping sand pies on the edge of the sand box, singing, "Pies, pies for sale, 50 cents a pie." The third child, while trading spoons with another, was not saying anything, she was just digging and digging in the sand.

As they grow and mature, children increasingly seek out peers to play with. Four- and five-year-olds engage in more group activity and are able to sustain a play theme playing cooperatively with others for a period of time. Five-year-olds will play fort, house, fire station or some other theme over a period of days. Even so, research suggests that children as old as 5 continue to spend about as much time in solitary and parallel play as they do in play with others (Berk, 2001).

Teachers of young children recognize that conflicts between children are frequent. Children fight over play objects, space, or nothing at all. Teachers can use a number of strategies to increase children's developing social skills:

- Asking children to recognize each other by looking at one another when talking and playing together
- Providing sufficient space and materials to avoid the potential for arguments and fights
- Ignoring small disruptions that children can solve themselves
- Modeling appropriate sharing and cooperative behaviors
- Providing other models whether through puppets, books, CDs, video clips, or other media of children getting along
- Teaching children the skills of how to enter a play group and leave peacefully, as well as other social skills

With increasing maturity and through social experiences, young children begin to realize that others have ideas and feelings, and they develop appropriate strategies for responding and relating to each other.

Culture

To know yourself and others is to know the culture you live in. The values and attitudes of a child's culture affect the growth and development of self-identity as well as determine the type of relationships a child will have with others. Think how the culture, with all of its shoulds and should nots, determines child-rearing practices.

Even before birth, the culture determines how pregnancy is treated. In some cultures pregnant women are segregated from society beginning at the seventh month of pregnancy. In other cultures, like that of the United States, pregnant women are supposed to continue their careers, travel, and be a vibrant part of society.

Babies born in some cultures sleep in their parents' bed; babies in other cultures sleep in their own bed away from their parents. One culture restricts the behavior of girls, another does not. One culture teaches children to respect adults by not making eye contact, and a different culture demands that children show their respect for adults by making eye contact. Children born into one culture are taught to eat with their right hands, while in another culture they are taught to use utensils, not hands, to eat.

Children born and raised in many different cultures are in today's child care and preschool programs. And they bring with them to the culture of the preschool program their own ways of knowing and behaving, those learned from the culture they were born and raised in. It is the teachers' job to

- Accommodate each child, and the culture they bring with them, into the child care setting
- Teach children to understand and respect the cultures of each other

Accommodation of and respect for each culture, while a complex process, can be built on a base of the universals of human development. For example, every child has a name, but how the name was chosen or should be used, may differ by culture. Teachers can make certain they know the proper names of children from other nations. They can use families as resources, asking family members which name is used informally and which name is the child's first name. If they are unfamiliar with how the name is pronounced, they can ask parents to help them practice saying the child's name until they master the sounds and patterns of the child's home language.

Each child has a birthday, but how birthdays are celebrated, or not celebrated, depends on the culture of the child. Each early childhood program also has a culture of birthdays. The point is to be able to respect the differing belief systems accompanying birthdays while transmitting the culture of the program and the United States. The families' practices can be incorporated into those of the programs.

In one center a family brought a small pumpkinlike squash stuffed with sweet rice pudding to send home with each child in celebration of their child's birthday. The child's mother explained the importance of the sweet rice pudding and told the story of the squash to the children. The treats were marveled over by children and families alike.

In addition to incorporating the family's customs into those of the center, many teachers have developed other ways of using children's birthdays. Concerned with the overblown birthday celebrations prevalent in the United States, some programs focus the birthday celebration on poems, stories, and mathematics. The poem by A. A. Milne, "Now We Are Six" (1955), is read and perhaps illustrated. Other stories about growth and development, such as Ruth Kraus's *The Growing Story* (1947), are read.

Of course, children sing "Happy Birthday." This is an opportune time to introduce musical notes. Make a music chart with the words and notes for "Happy Birthday," giving children an opportunity to learn about musical notation while singing a well-loved and very familiar song.

In some classes, the birthday child is asked to pick children to help with a special task. A 3-year-old is asked to pick three children, a 4-year-old, four children, and so on. Sometimes, the numeral representing the age of the birthday child is written on a hat for the child to wear during the day. Or the birthday child is asked to count out three, four, or five crackers or celery sticks for each child, whatever age the child is.

One center asks families to purchase a new book for the birthday child to give to the center. The birthday child tells the others why she or he selected the book and something about the book.

Besides names and birthdays, there are many other universals of human development that can serve as the foundation from which children learn how similar humans are regardless of their culture, and yet how diverse. Every human culture has some form of the following:

- *The arts.* Each culture has visual arts, music, dance, and theatre. Displaying art from the children's diverse cultures and using the same techniques to create art in the classroom acquaints children with the diversity of art. Likewise, each culture has music and theatre that can be showcased in the preschool.
- *Literature.* Reading myths or telling oral histories derived from the different cultures of the children introduces them to the idea that literature is universal, yet different. You might find different versions of the story of the Three Billy Goats Gruff, the Ginger Bread Boy, or the Three Little Pigs to read to the children. Children can then discuss how the versions of the same stories are alike and different.
- *Games.* The games of tag and hopscotch are found in many cultures. Ask children from other cultures to teach children how they play these games and compare them to the way the game is played in the preschool. Family members from the various cultures are the experts who teach the teacher and children to play their versions of Cat's Cradle and Duck, Duck, Goose, or how they played Cootie without the fancy plastic parts.
- *Shelter and clothing.* Brophy and Alleman (2002) argue that the cultural universals of the need for clothing

and shelter can be developed into rich, meaningful units of study that involve young children's minds and hands in grappling with the big ideas of cultural universals. The authors illustrate children's existing knowledge of these universals, and suggest ways for expanding and extending their knowledge. They advocate a powerful curriculum that integrates the idea that all people everywhere have needs for shelter and clothing into the fields of cultural literacy, history, and geography. They also advocate an issues analysis approach, within which children would investigate their own clothing and shelter, exploring how these universals are similar and different within their own classroom. Then, as the children grow and mature, the study is expanded to clothing and shelters used in other geographic locations and why or how these universals were manifested in past times.

See Figure 10.2 for assessing children's cultural awareness.

TIME, CHANGE, AND CONTINUITY

The social studies standards for history call for children to *develop a sense of time, ideas of change, and an understanding of the continuity of life.* As humans, we try to understand ourselves through our historic roots and to locate ourselves in time (NCSS, 1994). We gain a measure of self-identity by answering the questions, "Who am I?" "What happened in my past?" and "How am I connected to those in the past?"

Even the very youngest child is familiar with concepts of time, continuity, and change. These concepts, however, are not in any way similar to those of an adult. Vygotsky (1986) might call children's concepts of time

Figure 10.2. Assessing Cultural Awareness

Observe children at work and at play. Note and record instances of children

- Inviting those just learning English or otherwise new to the group into their play and activities

- Calling each other by their correct names

- Beginning to become aware of stereotypes in stories, greeting cards, and other media

- Entering into sociodramatic play using materials and props from other cultures

- Learning songs, poems, and chants from other cultures

and change embryonic and informal. Children understand the past as "a long time ago," which could refer to yesterday or to something that happened before they were born. They hold onto the idea that the biggest person in a group has to be the oldest, or that they can catch up in age to an older child as they grow. Regardless, teachers begin building on children's existing sense of the past.

Time

The predictable routines of the day form the basis for learning about time, continuity, and change. Three-year-old Tommy demonstrated how routines help children develop a sense of time and its passage. When someone asked him what time it was, Tommy said, "I don't know, but I know that after nap my daddy will come and get me."

Time can be measured through photos of children at work and play. Looking at photos taken the previous day enables children as young as age 3 to think about their immediate past and plan for the future. Two girls built a tower of blocks. As they looked at the digital photo the teacher had taken of their building after center time, they made plans for the next day. "Tomorrow," Alice told Sue, "we'll add another building, a long tunnel, then we'll make a wall all around."

Books about the passage of time can be selected. Teachers can read children factual books that describe what people do at night and during the day, or explain how some animals sleep during the night while others use the night to gather food, or show children going through a day and night. Children could create books of what they do throughout a day. Children like flip books, divided in half, with one side illustrating day and the other night (Seefeldt & Galper, 2000).

Children can begin to measure time as well. Hour glasses are enjoyed, with children seeing if they can complete a task—perhaps how many times they can jump or hop on one foot—before the sand runs out of the top of the glass. Kitchen timers could be set to help children remember when they need to begin cleaning up, or how much longer they can play outside. Providing stopwatches on the play yard prompts children to measure all kinds of activities. How long it takes them to climb to the top of the monkey bars, the time they each have to use a new or favorite piece of equipment, or how fast they can run. The watches do not have to be accurate; it is only the idea that time can be measured that is important.

Change

Things change over time. Children themselves offer numerous opportunities for the study of change over time. Just as every child needs a baby book, so does each child need a book of their months in a preschool program. Doubling as a history lesson and an assessment tool, each child's book could include photos of the child taken at the beginning and end of the year, charts of the child's height and weight, work samples collected at the beginning and end of the year. Narratives and anecdotes recorded throughout the year complete the book. Using the books, teachers ask children to

- Look at the photo of themselves arriving at school for the first day and tell how they felt
- Recall what they were thinking of when they drew or painted a picture included in the book
- Look at their growth chart and talk about how they've changed over the year
- List things they can do at the end of the year that they could not do at the beginning of the year
- Talk about what they learned and what they will learn in the future

Class history books are also valuable in developing children's sense of change over time. These books could be started during morning meeting at the beginning of the year. During the year, children could contribute a page about a favorite event or of something they learned to do that they could not do at the beginning of the year. Photos of children, the classroom, and the play yard

New equipment changed the play yard.

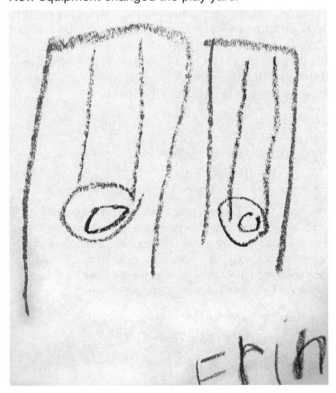

throughout the year add opportunities for children to describe how they and their school changed over time (Seefeldt, 2005).

Change occurs in plants and animals as well. One class charted the changes that took place in a crab apple tree on the play yard. Throughout the year children took photos of the tree ready to bud, in full bloom, after the leaves fell, and during the winter when the red crab apples served as food for birds. The class that raised mealworms studied the changes that occurred in the worms over a few weeks (see Chapter 6).

Continuity

The growth and change in children's families are the focus of other investigations of change and continuity. Photos of parents at the same age as their children can be examined and wondered over. A bulletin board of photos of the teachers as babies for children to match with current photos of their teachers is enjoyed by children and adults alike. The point is that although humans grow, develop, and change, they are still the same people.

Families demonstrate change and continuity. Not only do family members grow, age, and change, relationships also change. New members join the family through birth or marriage, others leave through divorce, moving away, or death. Yet, despite the changes, there is continuity within the family. The core values of the family—the love and respect for each other, the ability to care for one another—remain stable. (See Figure 10.3.)

The National Center for History in the Schools (1994) recommends the use of narratives to teach children about the continuity of life. Historical narratives offer believable accounts of human events. To listen to or read and understand narratives, biographies, or autobiographies, children must develop the ability to think imaginatively, to take into account what the story reveals about the individuals involved—their hopes, fears, intentions, and so on. Historic maps, artifacts, and a wide range of visual sources ranging from old photos, diaries, and paintings to videos, can supplement and help children elaborate on the information presented in narratives (NCHS, 1994). (See Figure 10.4 for assessment of children's concepts of time, change, and continuity.)

PEOPLE, PLACES, AND ENVIRONMENT

The social studies standards for geography state that children will *develop knowledge that the earth is the place they live.* This knowledge includes *recognizing a variety of surfaces that cover the earth and earth forms.* Children will *compare how they and others travel on the earth* and *become acquainted with maps and their use.*

Figure 10.3. Making the Home-School Connection (History)

There is continuity of human traditions. Send a note home, suggesting that families

- Read stories they loved as children to their own children

- Teach children to play the games they enjoyed playing

- Sing songs they loved as children

- Tell children the meaning of a treasured object or item

- Talk about what foods they liked as children and those they did not like

- Discuss how they felt and what they did on the first day of school

- Tell children about their childhood friends and what they are doing now

Swinging up and down, climbing to the top of the jungle gym, or crawling under a sheet tent in their classroom, children are developing initial foundational concepts of spatial knowledge and geographic perspectives. Through their sensorimotor experiences and other experiences in their here-and-

Figure 10.4. Assessing the Concepts of Time, Change, and Continuity

Observe children during the day and note when they are able to

- Know and follow established routines of the day

- Begin initial and arbitrary (nonstandard) measure of time

- Use time words such as *day* and *night*, *morning* and *afternoon*

- Talk about changes in themselves

- Recognize that their parents and teachers were once children

- Begin to generalize that although they, their families, and schools change, there is continuity to human life

now world, children can fulfill the national geographic concept standards, as explained in the sections that follow and in the "Sample Investigation" at the end of the chapter.

Concepts of the Earth

Children learn about the earth as the place they live simply by living on the earth. As they walk to school, climb a hill, or travel to another place, children are becoming acquainted with the features of the earth.

Explore the places where children live and play. What makes these places unique? Are the surfaces of the earth covered with water, sand, or concrete? With the goal of describing the places children live, the class can take walks around the school to name and describe, not only the differing surfaces of the earth, but how people use the characteristics of the place they live to create shelters or adapt to the weather of the place. Ask children to utilize their skills of observing, collecting, and analyzing information as they explore the surfaces of their earth and differing landforms (Fromboluti & Seefeldt, 1999). (See Figure 10.5 for ways to involve families in exploring the earth.)

Teachers can use books, pictures, charts, video clips, and CDs to teach children vocabulary about the earth. Viewing visuals gives children the opportunity to learn words such as *waves*, *oceans*, *desert*, and *mountain*.

Computer technology can be utilized to increase children's ideas of the earth around them and far away. Through the use of *Journey North* (Annenberg/CPB, 2004) children become aware of landforms they cannot directly experience. How the landforms shape human life is made clear through their interactions with children, just like them, who happen to live in different areas of the world (see also Chapter 3).

Figure 10.5. Making the Home-School Connection (Geography)

Send a note home asking families to point out and talk about the different forms of land and water they observe. Families may travel to mountains, through the flat prairie lands, to the seashore or lake, or spend time on a river. Throughout their travels, families can introduce children to new vocabulary. They might name:

Hills, flatlands, meadows, mountains

Ponds, lakes, oceans

Streams, creeks, rivers

Children Travel on the Earth

Teachers can ask children to explore how many ways they can move on the earth. Start with asking them how many ways they can move their bodies to cover space. Then ask children to run as fast as they can and stop on a given signal. Have them try exploring running through the grass, on a hard surface, and on sand or gravel. Compare which surface is the smoothest and easiest to run on.

There are other ways of moving on this earth as well. Children can crawl, hop, skip, walk, or jump. Or teachers can ask children to work with a partner and find a different way of moving over the earth. (See Figure 10.6 for integrating geography and language learning.)

Figure 10.6. Directional Vocabulary

As children explore how they move over the surfaces of the earth, teachers can introduce directional vocabulary. Children learn that they can:

Run *up* and *down* hills

Move *forward*, *backward*, or *sidewards*

Crawl *in*, *out*, *through*, *under*, and *over* objects on the play yard

---

Providing children with a variety of wheeled toys gives them other experiences with traveling on their earth. Trikes, wagons, carts, and other wheeled vehicles can be compared and contrasted for their ability to move over different surfaces and around obstacles.

If your school is located near a street, children can observe the variety of vehicles that pass by the school. If not, walk to a busier corner, complete with clipboards and markers, to record the number and types of trucks, buses, and other vehicles that pass by. Speculate on the purpose of different trucks and carriers, where they are going and who can drive them. Back in the classroom construct a graph of common vehicles observed.

Continue the study of moving across the earth by asking children to graph how they arrive at the school. Graph the number who walk, ride in cars, take a bus, or car pool.

Maps

Even though maps—abstract and complicated representations of the earth—are far beyond children's understandings, they belong in good schools for young children. A variety of maps should be provided for

Carts are made and their speed studied.

children's play. Board games often are based on a semblance of a map; small area rugs may depict maps; puzzles may represent maps; and maps are found in children's picture books.

Collect small maps for children's use in the housekeeping and outdoor vehicle play area. You can find these at local malls, parks, shopping centers, and other

Mapping the world with blocks.

area attractions. Try to find maps that represent a place familiar to children and that use pictures to represent places. Children will play with these maps as they chart and plan trips. Use maps as you take field trips. Draw small maps of where you are going and copy the map so children can follow along.

Be sure to place maps with the blocks. A box of wooden animals, people, and vehicles, along with strips of brown wrapping paper that children use to represent roads and pieces of blue paper representing ponds, lakes, and rivers, stimulate children building dioramas of places they have been or can only image.

Children have been found to draw and make maps before they can actually read maps. You could involve children in redesigning the play yard or room. With large pieces of paper and markers or objects representing play equipment or furniture, children can draw or move objects on the paper to create their idea of the best arrangement for the play yard or room.

Stories could lead children to creating imaginary maps. For example, where do the wild things live in *Where the Wild Things Are* (Sendak, 1988)? Children could draw maps of how the wild things find their home again. Or children can draw maps of where the Gingerbread Boy ran, of Sam's trip to the jungle where the tigers were in *Sam and the Tigers* (Lester, 2003), or a map of the path Little Red Riding Hood took through the woods.

One first-grade teacher collected small milk cartons. The children covered these with construction paper to create their houses. Each house was mounted on a sheet of paper, on which children drew the school, and then the map to their house. They completed their maps by writing their address and phone number on their maps.

PRODUCTION AND CONSUMPTION

The social studies standards for economics indicate that children are to become aware of the basic principle of economics, that there is a difference between *wants and needs*. During the early years children can also become aware of the concepts of *producers and consumers*.

Who hasn't heard a child ask for "more"? The differences between want and need are at the heart of economics education. Children who understand the concepts of want and need are those who will be able to make wise economic decisions, choosing to save, conserve, produce, and consume with care.

Limiting the commercial aspects of the early childhood setting is one way to introduce children to the idea of want and need. Teachers ask themselves, What do children really need? Do they need the fancy climbing gym? Or do they need a place to run and an obstacle course of empty cardboard boxes or large wooden blocks? True, the very expensive kitchen furniture ad-

vertised at a popular store is appealing. But do children need this, or do they need a set of large hollow blocks from which to make their own sink, stove, and table?

Without commercial items, children are forced to use their imaginations and problem-solving skills. At the Center for Young Children at the University of Maryland in College Park, children use hollow blocks to represent the housekeeping area, a store, plant nursery, or post office. They are the ones who determine their goal, communicate the goal to others, negotiate and problem solve, as they create a multitude of play spaces. Materials are limited as well. It's not that children can not choose from a wide range of papers, paints, paste, and other art materials, but children are taught to save paper scraps in a clear plastic box for use at another time, and to think about the size and type of paper they really need for a project.

Children's literature is useful in promoting the idea of wants and needs (VanFossen, 2003). *If You Give a Mouse a Cookie* (Numeroff, 1985), the story of a mouse and cookie that starts a chain of events introduces the idea of limited wants, goods, and services. Other books, such as *Alexander, Who Used to be Rich Last Sunday* (Viorst, 1978) and *Bunny Money* (Wells, 1997), convey the idea of money and its uses.

In addition to the idea that there are limited goods and services and unlimited wants, there are the concepts of producers and consumers. Young children can experience both concepts within their school (see Figure 10.7). Children can be asked to produce art, stories, songs, dances, and plays for others. Gifts are produced for others, either by individual children or by the group. As individuals, children can

- Make a frame from a box lid for a special drawing or picture to give to a family member or friend
- Plant seeds in a pot and give the growing plant as a gift
- Mount a photograph in a construction paper frame to give to a grandparent

As a group, children can

- Produce cookies, with each taking over a part of the cookie-making and packing process
- Create a play to put on for younger or older children in the school
- Write a group story and publish it to distribute to each family

CIVIC IDEALS AND PRACTICES

Standards for civic ideals and practices call for children to become participatory citizens of a democratic

Figure 10.7. Sociodramatic Play: Producers and Consumers

Setting up a variety of sociodramatic play areas lets children reenact their investigations of a shoe, grocery, or plant store (Seefeldt & Galper, 2000).

- Hollow blocks are available to build the store.

- The store is equipped with appropriate props:
  * *A shoe store*—shoes, foot-measuring tools, play money
  * *A grocery store*—paper receipt tape, play money, bags, boxes, cans of food
  * *A plant nursery*—cash register tape, pots and plants, boxes, and seeds

The following all-purpose items are provided for the play areas:

- Nonstereotypic clothing for various jobs

- Props such as stamps, ink pads, bins and boxes for holding goods

- Charts and clipboards for recording job performance and other details

- Photographs of people at work

- Bins and boxes for materials to be recycled or reused

---

society. To do so, children will learn to *care for themselves, give up some of their individuality for the good of the group, and vote and follow the will of the majority.*

Within their own small democracy of the classroom, children can learn civic ideals and practices. From a base of security and a foundation of trust, children learn to care for themselves and their own things. Even the youngest children are given responsibility for learning to care for themselves. Children sign their names on the chart telling who is in the group today. Or they take their photo from a stack and place it on the We Are Here Chart. Children are taught how to care for their clothing, where and how to hang their coats and sweaters, and where and how to place other items they bring from home or will take home with them at the end of the day.

Children are helped to dress and undress themselves. "You pull the heel, and I'll push the sock on your foot," said one teacher helping a 2-year-old achieve the difficult task of dressing himself.

At the same time that children are learning to care for themselves, they assume partial responsibility for the care of others. Instead of cleaning up after children, teachers help children to clean up after themselves. Tables are washed, crumbs brushed up, and sinks and faucets wiped clean. Tooth brushes and paste are kept in their containers.

Teachers should ask children to make many choices for themselves and to think about their choices. Some children may need help in making choices. They might ask, "What should I do?" "Is this right?" Reassure these children that they can decide for themselves. Perhaps offer them two acceptable choices, "You can begin with the blocks or at the art table."

Whenever possible for special tasks, give children an opportunity to choose. You might ask a child to select two or three others to walk with him to the director's office, or to deliver a gift to the cook. Children can pick others to sing with them, read with them, or play with them.

Children also learn to give up some of their own desires to follow the will of the group. Doing so starts gradually. First voting experiences involve all children, and each child is able to experience his or her choice. After reading "The King's Breakfast" (Milne, 1969) children voted on whether they wanted to have butter or marmalade on their bread. Each child tasted the marmalade and butter and made his or her own choice. Children could vote to play either Duck, Duck, Goose or Farmer in the Dell and then play the game they voted for. Similarly, when making pudding, let each child select either chocolate or vanilla.

After many experiences with voting and being able to receive his or her choice, children move to voting as a group and following the will of the group. By the end of kindergarten or beginning of first grade, children will be able to understand that if the majority of children vote for chocolate pudding, the treat will be chocolate pudding that day.

IN SUMMARY

- The social studies are comprised of a wide variety of separate subject matter disciplines.
- The standards represent content from culture, history, geography, knowledge of self and others, social skills, economics, and civic participation.
- Self-identity and knowledge of others go hand in hand and are integrated within the total curriculum.
- Cultural awareness takes place through study of the universals of human development—children's birthdays, clothing, art, and music.
- The study of history—time, change, and continuity—takes place through study of children's lives.
- Concepts of place and geography are investigated through study of children's here-and-now world.
- Economic concepts of wants and needs and producers and consumers are embedded in the total curriculum.

- Children develop civic responsibility and participation by learning to care for themselves and others within the small democracy of their classrooms.

SAMPLE INVESTIGATION: CHILDREN STUDY THEIR PLAY YARD

Geography

Being out of doors is different than being inside. Outdoors children are in a natural environment. They're surrounded with opportunities to learn about their physical world and be introduced to concepts from the field of geography. Children can study the surfaces of the earth, what they do on the earth, and concepts of maps.

Selected Standards

Develop knowledge of different earth surfaces and how the differences affect activities.
Make and use maps.

Activities

Toddlers (two–three years old). Toddlers can learn the nature and names of the surfaces of the earth by experiencing them. Actually touching, feeling, and at the same time talking about the surfaces of the earth is the only way toddlers have of learning.

- Informally, talk about the surfaces covering the play yard.
- Again, using the teachable moment, when children are involved yet open to talking, name the surfaces of the yard. "Ride your trike here, on the blacktop. See how much easier it is to ride your bike on the blacktop than in the grass."
- Digging is a great activity for toddlers. They love the repetitive fill and spill aspects of digging in the sand or dirt. As they do so, they are being introduced to the properties of the surfaces of their earth. Add squirt bottles of water so children can see what happens to sand and dirt when it's wet.

Preschoolers (three–four years old). Preschoolers can expand their ideas about the surfaces of the earth. Preschoolers, however, are still in the preoperational stage of thought. They think the earth made itself (Piaget, 1969), or think the sand was made so they can play with it. Keeping in mind children's thinking, you can extend and expand their understanding of the surfaces of the earth as well as their vocabulary.

Children explore their earth.

- Ask the children to observe what happens to the surfaces of the yard after a rain. Have them look for puddles and slippery surfaces. Point out how the grass seems to catch drops of rain on the tips of the blades.

Kindergarten children (four–five years old). Kindergarten children are able to be introduced to maps and explore the surfaces of the play yard in depth.

- Begin the study of mapping. After the children have measured all sides of the play yard, ask them to focus their observations on where items of play yard equipment, trees, plants, and other markers are located. As they identify things on the yard, draw a map of the play yard. Explain to children that this map is smaller than the play yard but will tell them where things are located.
- To further children's understanding of maps, hide a toy under or around a piece of equipment. Divide the class into small groups, and give each group a map with an *X* marking the spot where a treasure is hidden. Together, each group solves the problem of how to find the hidden toy.
- Have children draw their own maps of the play yard and their classroom. Or children could use blocks to build a representation of their play yard and classroom.
- On another day ask children to explore the different surfaces of their play yard. Give them clipboards and markers to record their findings. Hold a group meeting and ask children to name the different surfaces.
- Now ask children to explore what activities they can do best on each of the surfaces. Record and categorize their answers. Then have children conduct some experiments:

1. Ride their trikes on the blacktop or concrete, stopping on a signal such as ringing a bell or clapping hands. Now take the hose and wet the blacktop. Repeat the experiment to see how fast they can stop their trikes when the top is wet. What makes the difference?
2. Bring blocks outside, and ask children to build on a smooth surface and on the grass. Ask them to build something as tall as they can. What happens to the buildings built on the grass and on the smooth surface?
3. Run on different surfaces of the play yard to determine which is best for running. Use a stopwatch to measure the time it takes to run across a stretch of grass, blacktop, or gravel. What do the children conclude?

Complete the experiments by asking children to draw themselves running, riding their trikes, and building on the different surfaces of the yard. Fives can begin writing their own labels using invented spelling. Mount the finished drawings on a bulletin board labeled "We Experiment" along with a description of the experiments completed.

Children travel on the earth.

Assessing Children's Learning

Observe

- Note vocabulary children use as they explore the surfaces of the earth. Are children discussing the properties of the earth when the earth is wet and dry?
- Pay attention to how children solve problems of riding, walking and running, or building on different surfaces of the earth.
- Notice children's play with maps and how they build maps when outside.

Interview

- Ask individual children to name different surfaces of the earth. Note and record the surfaces they can name.
- Ask children to describe and discuss different surfaces of the earth. Note and record how complete and accurate children's concepts of different surfaces are.

Assign a task to perform

- Give older children a map of the play yard. Ask them to name landmarks on the map, and walk to the places on the play yard.
- Ask children to draw a map of their play yard.

Analyze children's work

- Review children's drawings of themselves running and playing outside several times over the year. Note increasing use of details, realism, and completeness.
- Examine children's spontaneous drawings of maps, noting increasing details and accuracy.

Resources

The standards in this book have been compiled from a number of resources. These resources and the organizations and associations that developed standards are listed below.

American Association for the Advancement of Science. (1989). *Science for all Americans.* New York: Oxford University Press.

American Association for the Advancement of Science. (1993). *Benchmarks for science literacy.* New York: Oxford University Press.

Bredekamp, S., & Copple, C. (Eds.). (1997). *Developmentally appropriate practices in early childhood programs* (Rev. ed.). Washington, DC: National Association for the Education of Young Children.

Bredekamp, S., & Rosegrant, T. (Eds.). (1992, 1997). *Reaching potentials: Appropriate curriculum and assessment for young children.* (Vols. 1–2). Washington, DC: National Association for the Education of Young Children.

Consortium of National Arts Education Associations. (1994). *Dance, music, theatre, visual arts: What every young American should know and be able to do in the arts: National standards for arts education.* Reston, VA; Music Educators National Conference.

Copley, J. V. (2000). *The young children and mathematics.* Washington, DC: National Association for the Education of Young Children.

Geography Education Standards Project. (1994). *Geography for life: National geography standards 1994.* Washington, DC: National Geographic Research & Exploration.

International Society for Technology in Education (ISTE). (2002). *National educational technology standards/NETS project.* Eugene, OR: Author.

Maryland State Department of Education. (1992). *Laying the foundation for school success.* Baltimore, MD: Author.

McLaughlin, B. (1995). *Fostering second language development in young children: Principles and practices* (Educational Practice Report No. 14). Washington, DC: National Center for Research on Cultural Diversity and Second Language Learning.

Music Educators National Conference. (1994). *MENC position statement on early childhood education.* Reston, VA: Author.

National Art Education Association. (1994). *Suggested policy perspectives on art content and student learning.* Reston, VA: Author.

National Association for the Education of Young Children. (1996). *Technology and young children.* Washington, DC: Author.

National Association for the Education of Young Children and International Reading Association. (1998). *Learning to read and write: A joint position statement of the International Reading Association and the National Association for the Education of Young Children.* Washington, DC: National Association for the Education of Young Children.

National Association for Sports and Physical Education. (2002). *Active start: Physical activity for children birth to five years.* Reston, VA: Author.

National Council of Teachers of English and the International Reading Association. (2003). *Standards for the English language arts.* Washington, DC: Authors.

National Council of Teachers of Mathematics (2000). *Principles and standards for school mathematics.* Reston, VA: Author.

National Council of Teachers of Mathematics and National Association for the Education of Young Children. (2002). *Learning paths and strategies in early mathematics.* Reston, VA: Authors.

National Research Council. (1996). *National science education standards.* Washington, DC: National Academy Press.

National Research Council. (1998). Accomplishments in reading. In *Preventing reading difficulties in young children* (p. 80, Table 2.2). Washington, DC: National Academy Press.

National Research Council. (2001). *Adding it up: Helping children learn mathematics.* Washington, DC: National Academy Press.

National Research Council. (2001). *Eager to learn: Educating our preschoolers.* Washington, DC: National Academy Press.

National Research Council and Institute of Medicine. (2000). *From neurons to neighborhoods: The science of early childhood development.* Washington, DC: National Academy Press.

National Standards in Foreign Language Education Project. (1996). *Standards for foreign language learning: Preparing for the twenty-first century*. Washington, DC: Author; Yonkers, NY: American Council on the Teaching of Foreign Languages.

Neuman, S. B., Copple, C., & Bredekamp, S. (2000). *Learning to read and write: Developmentally appropriate practices for young children*. Washington, DC: National Association for the Education of Young Children.

New Standards. (1999). *Reading and writing grade by grade: Primary literacy standards*. Pittsburgh, PA: University of Pittsburgh.

Pennsylvania Department of Education and Pennsylvania Association of Intermediate Units. (2002). *Early childhood learning continuum indicators*. Harrisburg, PA: Pennsylvania Department of Education.

Sandall, S., McLean, M., & Smith, B. J. (Eds.). (2000). *DEC recommended practices in early intervention/Early childhood special education*. Denver, CO: Division for Early Childhood (DEC) of the Council for Exceptional Children (CEC).

Strickland, D. S., & Morrow, L. M. (2000). *Beginning reading and writing*. New York: Teachers College Press.

Teachers of English to Speakers of Other Languages (TESOL). (2001). *ESL standards for pre-K–12*. Alexandria, VA: Author.

Texas State Department of Education. (2001). *Prekindergarten curriculum guidelines*. Dallas, TX: Author.

U. S. Department of Education. (2001). *Building strong foundations for early learning*. Washington, DC: Author.

U.S. Department of Health and Human Services. (2000). *Head Start child outcomes framework*. Washington, DC: Author.

References

Achilles, E. (1994). Creating music environments in early childhood programs. *Young Children, 54*(1), 21–26.

Adams, M. J. (1990). *Beginning to read: Thinking and learning about print.* Cambridge, MA: MIT Press.

Agape Press. (2004). Today's news summary. Retrieved November 3, 2004, from Agape Press Web site: http://www.agapepress.org

Althouse, R., Johnson, M. H., & Mitchell, S. T. (2003). *The colors of learning: Integrating the visual arts into the early childhood curriculum.* New York: Teachers College Press.

American Association of University Women (AAUW). (1998). *Gender gaps: Where schools still fail our children.* Washington, DC: American Association of University Women Educational Foundation.

American Federation of Teachers (AFT). (1996). *Implementing Goals 2000.* Washington, DC: Author.

Annenberg/CPB. (2004). *Journey north.* Retrieved November 3, 2004, from http://www.leaner.org/jnorth/

Association for Childhood Education International (ACEI). (1998). *Preparation of early childhood education teachers.* Olney, MD: Author.

Bailey, H., & Huszan, S. (1998). *The playground.* Toronto: Annick Press.

Barbarin, O. A. (2002). The Black-White achievement gap in early reading skills: Familial and socio-cultural context. In B. Bowman (Ed.), *Love to read: Essays in developing and enhancing early literacy skills of African American children.* Washington, DC: National Black Child Development Institute, Inc.

Barbour, C., & Barbour, N. (1997). *Families, schools and communities: Building partnerships.* Upper Saddle River, NJ: Merrill.

Baroody, A. J., & Wilkins, J. L. M. (1999). The development of informal counting, number and arithmetic skills and concepts. In J. V. Copley (Ed.), *Mathematics in the early years* (pp. 48–65). Reston, VA: National Council of Teachers of Mathematics; Washington, DC: National Association for the Education of Young Children.

Bear, D. R., & Templeton, S. (1998). Explorations in developmental spelling: Foundations for learning and teaching phonics, spelling, and vocabulary. *The Reading Teacher, 52,* 222–242.

Bereiter, C., & Engelmann, S. (1966). *Teaching disadvantaged children in the preschool.* Englewood Cliffs, NJ: Prentice-Hall.

Berk, L. E. (2001). *Development through the lifespan* (2nd ed.). Boston: Allyn & Bacon.

Bodrova, E., & Leong, D. J. (2003). Building language and literacy through play. *Early Childhood Today, 18*(2), 34–38.

Bodrova, E., & Leong, D. J., Paynter, D. E., & Semenov, D. (2000). *A framework for early literacy instruction: Aligning standards to developmental accomplishments and student behaviors.* Aurora, CO: Mid-continent Research for Education and Learning.

Bredekamp, S. (1987). *Developmentally appropriate practice in early childhood programs serving children from birth through age 8.* Washington, DC: National Association for the Education of Young Children.

Bredekamp, S. [et al.]. (1998). *The leading edge: Tools for teaching developmentally appropriate practice* [videotapes]. Washington, DC: National Association for the Education of Young Children.

Bredekamp, S., & Copple, C. (Eds.). (1997). *Developmentally appropriate practice in early childhood programs* (Rev. ed.). Washington, DC: National Association for the Education of Young Children.

Bredekamp, S., & Rosegrant, T. (Eds.). (1992, 1997). *Reaching potentials: Appropriate curriculum and assessment for young children* (Vols. 1–2). Washington, DC: National Association for the Education of Young Children.

Brophy, J., & Alleman, J. (2002). Beyond expanding horizons: New curriculum directions for elementary social studies. *Elementary School Journal, 103,* 99–114.

Bruner, J. (1966). *Toward a theory of instruction.* Cambridge, MA: Belknap Press.

Bruna, D. (1996). *Miffy at the playground.* New York: Kodansha International.

Burns, M. S., Bodrova, E., Leong, D. J., & Midgette, E. (2001). *Prekindergarten benchmarks for early learning.* Unpulished manuscript, George Mason University, Fairfax, VA.

Center for Civic Education (CCE). (1994). *National standards for civics and government.* Calabasas, CA: Author.

Christie, J., Enz, B., & Vukelich, C. (1997). *Teaching language and literacy.* New York: Longman.

Clay, M. M. (1979). *Concepts about print test.* Portsmouth, NH: Heinemann.

Coakley, M. C. (1997). Using arts in early intervention programs: Long-term outcomes. *Dissertation Abstracts International, 61,* 2B. (Publication No. AAT9962108).

Consortium of National Arts Education Associations (CNAEA). (1994). *Dance, music, theatre, visual arts: What every young American should know and be able to do in the arts: National standards for arts education.* Reston, VA: Music Edu-cators National Conference. (Also available online at ArtsEdge Web site: http://artsedge.kennedy-center. org/teach/standards/)

Cooper, J. L., & Dever, M. T. (2001). Sociodramatic play as a vehicle for curriculum integration in first grade. *Young Children, 56*(3), 58–60.

Copley, J. V. (2000). *The young child and mathematics.* Washington, DC: National Association for the Education of Young Children.

Council for Basic Education (CBE). (1998). *Standards for excellence in education: A guide for parents, teachers, and principals for evaluating and implementing standards for education.* Washington, DC: Author.

CTB/McGraw-Hill. (2002). *Pre-K standards: Guidelines for teaching and learning.* Retrieved November 5, 2004, from CTB/McGraw-Hill Web site [Resources]: http://www: CTB.com

De la Mare, W. (1961). *Tom Tiddler's ground; A book of poetry for children.* New York: Knopf.

Dewey, J. (1910). *How we think.* New York: D. C. Heath.

Dewey, J. (1944). *Democracy and education.* New York: Free Press.

Dodge, D. T., Heroman, C., Charles, J., & Maiorca, J. (2004). Beyond outcomes: How ongoing assessment supports children's learning and leads to meaningful curriculum. *Young Children, 59*(1), 20–29.

Dolezal, S. E., Welsh, L. M., & Pressley, M. (2003). How nine third-grade teachers motivate student academic engagement. *Elementary School Journal, 103,* 239–267.

Douglas, N., & Schwartz, J. (1967). Increasing awareness of art ideas of young children through guided experiences with ceramics. *Studies in Art Education, 15*(2), 2–9.

Durrell, D. D. (1963). Success in first-grade reading. *Journal of Education, 148,* 1–8.

Dyson, A. H. (1993). *Social worlds of children learning to write in an urban primary school.* New York: Teachers College Press.

Epstein, A. (2001). Thinking about art: Encouraging art appreciation in early childhood settings. *Young Children, 56*(3), 38–43.

Epstein, A. (2003). How planning and reflection develop young children's thinking skills. *Young Children, 58*(5), 28–36.

Fromboulti, C., & Seefeldt, C. (1999). *Early childhood: Where learning begins: Geography.* Washington, DC: U.S. Department of Education.

Gardiner, M. F., Fox, A., Knowles, F., & Jeffrey, D. (1996). Learning improved by arts training. *Nature, 381*(6580), 284.

Gelman, S. (1995). How does your garden grow? Early concepts of seeds and their place in the plant growth cycle. *Child Development, 66*(3), 856–876.

Geography Education Standards Project (GESP). (1994). *Geography for life: National geography standards 1994.* Washington, DC: National Geographic Research & Exploration (NGRE).

Goals 2000: Educate America Act, 20 U.S.C. Sec. 5801 *et.seq.* (1994). Available online: http://www.ed.gov/legislation/GOALS2000/theAct/index.html

Gorski, P. G. (2003). Pedagogy, politics, and schools—III. *Multicultural Education, 10*(4), 61–63.

Halpern, D. (2004). I dare you to try this at home (or at work). *APA Monitor on Psychology, 35*(2), 5.

Harlan, J. D., & Rivkin, M. S. (2004). *Science experiences in the early years.* Upper Saddle River, NJ: Prentice/Merrill.

Hatch, J. A. (2002). Accountability showdown: Resisting the standards movement in early childhood education. *Phi Delta Kappan, 83,* 457–462.

Hawkins, M. R. (2004). Researching English language and literacy development in schools. *Educational Researcher, 33*(4), 1–14.

Helm, J. H., & Beneke, S. (Eds.). (2003). *The power of projects.* New York: Teachers College Press.

Helm, J. H., & Katz, L. (2001). *Young investigators: The project approach in the early years.* New York: Teachers College Press.

Henderson, J. G. (2001). Deepening democratic curriculum work. *Educational Researcher, 9*(30), 18–22.

Hill, P. S. (1902). The value of constructive work in the kindergarten. *Proceedings of the Ninth Convention of the International Kindergarten Union,* pp. 107–135.

Hogg, J., & McWhinnie, H. (1968). A pilot research in aesthetic education. *Studies in Art Education, 9*(2), 52–60.

Hughes, E. (2002). Planning meaningful curriculum: A mini story of children and teachers learning together. *Childhood Education, 78,* 134–139.

Hughes, M. (1934). *A unit of work: Carrying the mail.* New York: Macmillian.

Humphreys, J. (2000). Exploring nature with young children. *Young Children, 55*(2), 16–22.

Hunt, J. M. (1961). *Intelligence and experience.* New York: Ronald Press.

Hyson, M. L. (Ed.) (2003). *Preparing early childhood professionals: NAEYC's Standards for initial licensure, advanced, and associate degree programs.* Washington, DC: National Association for the Education of Young Children.

Jones, J., & Courtney, R. (2002). Documenting early science learning. *Young Children, 57*(5), 34–38.

Kagan, S. L., & Scott-Little, C. (2004). Early learning standards: Changing the parlance and practice of early childhood education? *Phi Delta Kappan, 85*(5), 388–396.

Kagan, S. L., Scott-Little, C., & Frelow, V. S. (2003). Early learning standards for young children: A survey of the states. *Young Children, 58*(5), 58–64.

Katz, L. (2003). Building a good foundation for children. In J. H. Helm & S. Beneke (Eds.), *The power of projects* (pp. 10–18). New York: Teachers College Press.

Kaye, B. (1998). *A, you're adorable.* New York: Candlewick Press.

Keats, E. J. (1963). *The snowy day.* New York: Viking Press.

Kendall, J. S., & Marzano, R. J. (2004). *Content knowledge: A compendium of standards and benchmarks for K–12 educa-*

tion. Aurora, CO: Mid-continent Research for Education and Learning (McREL). Online database: http://www.mcrel.org/standards-benchmarks/

Kraus, R. (1947). *The growing story*. New York: HarperCollins.

Lawrence-Lightfoot, S. (2003). *The essential conversation: What parents and teachers can learn from each other*. New York: Random House.

Lester, J. (2003). *Sam and the tigers: A new telling of Little Black Sambo*. New York: Bt Bound.

Lewis, A. (2003). Educating our youngest citizens. *Phi Delta Kappan, 85*(2), 99–101.

Linn, R. (2003). *Constructs and values in standards based assessment*. Mahwah, NJ: Lawrence Erlbaum.

Lortie, D. C. (1975). *Schoolteacher*. Chicago: University of Chicago Press.

Mager, R. (1962). *Preparing instructional objectives*. Palo Alto, CA: Fearon.

Martin, B. (1969). *Good night, Mrs. Beetle*. New York: Holt, Rinehart & Winston.

Martin, M. O., & Kelly, D. L. (1998). *Third International Mathematics and Science Study (TIMSS): Technical report* (Vols. 1–3). Chestnut Hill, MA: Boston College.

Marzano, R. J. (2002). *Curriculum and instruction: Critical and emerging issues for educational research*. Aurora, CO: Mid-continent Research for Education and Learning (McREL).

Mayer, R. E. (2004). Should there be a three-strikes rule against discovery learning? *American Psychologist, 59*(1), 14–19.

Meisels, S. J. (1993). Remaking classroom assessment with the Work Sampling System. *Young Children, 48*(5), 34–41.

Meisels, S. J., & Atkins-Burnett, S. (2004). The Head Start National Reporting System: A critique. *Young Children, 59*(1), 64–66.

Meisels, S. J., Liaw, E., Dorfman, A., & Nelson, R. F. (1995). The Work Sampling System: Reliability and validity of a performance assessment for young children. *Early Childhood Research Quarterly, 10*, 277–296.

Meisels, S. J., Xue, Y., Bickel, D., Nicholson, J., & Atkins-Burnett, S. (2001). Parental reactions to authentic performance assessment. *Educational Assessment, 7*(1), 61–85.

Milne, A. A. (1955). The king's breakfast. In *Now we are six*. London: Dutton.

Milne, A. A. (1955). Now we are six. In *Now we are six*. London: Dutton.

Mitchell, L. S. (1934). *Young Geographers*. New York: Bank Street College.

National Assessment of Educational Progress (NAEP). (1996). *Mathematics framework for the 1996 National Assessment of Educational Progress*. Washington, DC: Author.

National Association for the Education of Young Children (NAEYC). (1986). *Good teaching practices for 4- and 5-year-olds: A position statement for the National Association for the Education of Young Children*. Washington, DC: National Association for the Education of Young Children.

National Association for the Education of Young Children (NAEYC). (1998). *Accreditation criteria and procedures of the National Association for the Education of Young Children*. Washington, DC: Author.

National Association for the Education of Young Children

(NAEYC) and National Association of Early Childhood Specialists in State Departments of Education (NAECS/SDE). (2003). *Early childhood curriculum, assessment and program evaluation: Building an effective, accountable system in programs for children birth through age 8*. Washington, DC: NAEYC.

National Center for Education Statistics (NCES). (2003). *Prekindergarten programs*. Retrieved on November 10, 2004, from http://nces.ed.gov/

National Center for History in the Schools (NCHS). (1996). *National standards for history*. Los Angeles: Author. Retrieved November 18, 2004, from http://nchs.ucla.edu/standards

National Commission on Excellence in Education. (1983). *A nation at risk: The imperative for educational reform*. Washington, DC: Author.

National Commission on Social Studies. (1989). *Charting a course: Social studies for the 21st century*. Washington, DC: Author.

National Council for the Social Studies (NCSS). (1988). *Social studies for early childhood and elementary school children: Preparing for the 21st century* [Position paper]. Retrieved November 10, 2004, from http://www.socialstudies.org/positions/elementary

National Council for the Social Studies (NCSS). (1994). *Expectations of excellence: Curriculum standards for social studies*. Silver Spring, MD: Author. Some parts are available online: http://www.socialstudies.org/standards/

National Council of Teachers of English (NCTE) and the International Reading Association (IRA). (1995). *Standards for the English language*. Washington, DC: Authors.

National Council of Teachers of English (NCTE) and International Reading Association (IRA). (2003). *Standards for the English language arts*. www:ncte.org.

National Council of Teachers of Mathematics (NCTM). (1989). *Curriculum and evaluation standards for school mathematics*. Reston, VA: Author.

National Council of Teachers of Mathematics (NCTM). (1991). *Curriculum and evaluation standards for school mathematics: Addenda series, grades K–6*. Reston, VA: Author.

National Council of Teachers of Mathematics (NCTM). (2000). *Principles and standards for school mathematics*. Reston, VA: Author. Retrieved November 19, 2004, from http://www.standards.nctm.org

National Council of Teachers of Mathematics (NCTM) and National Association for the Education of Young Children (NAEYC). (2002). *Learning paths and strategies in early mathematics*. Reston, VA: Authors.

National Education Goals Panel (NEGP). (1991, 1994). *Goals 2000*. Washington, DC: Author.

National Education Goals Panel (NEGP). (1991). *The National Education Goals report: Building a nation of learners*. Washington, DC: U.S. Government Printing Office.

National Education Goals Panel (NEGP). (1994). *The National Education Goals report: Building a nation of learners*. Washington, DC: U.S. Government Printing Office.

National Research Council (NRC). (2001a). *Adding it up: Helping children learn mathematics*. Washington, DC: National Academy Press.

National Research Council (NRC). (2001b). *Eager to learn:*

Educating our preschoolers. Washington, DC: National Academy Press.

National Research Council (NRC) and Institute of Medicine (IOM). (2000). *From neurons to neighborhoods: The science of early childhood development*. Washington, DC: National Academy Press.

National Research Council (NRC) and National Academy of Science (NAS). (1996). *National science education standards: Observe, interact, change, learn*. Washington, DC: National Academy Press.

Neuman, S. , Copple, C., & Bredekamp, S. (2000). *Learning to read and write: Developmentally appropriate practices for young children*. Washington, DC: National Association for the Education of Young Children.

New Standards. (1999). *Reading and writing grade by grade: Primary literacy standards*. Pittsburgh, PA: University of Pittsburgh.

No Child Left Behind Act (NCLB), 20 U.S.C. Sec. 6301 *et seq.* (2002). Available online: http://www.ed.gov/policy/elsec/leg/esea02/index.html

Numeroff, L. J. (1985). *If you give a mouse a cookie*. New York: Geringer.

Oakes, J., Quartz, K., Ryan, S., & Lipton, M. (2000). *Becoming good American schools: The struggle for civic virtue in education reform*. San Francisco: Jossey-Bass.

Pastnaik, J. (2003). Learning about the other. *Childhood Education, 79*, 204–211.

Piaget, J. (1969). *The psychology of the child*. New York: Basic Books.

Popkewitz, T. (2004). The alchemy of the mathematics curriculum: Inscriptions and the fabrication of the child. *American Educational Research Journal, 41*, 3–35.

Porter, A. C. (2002). Measuring the content of instruction: Uses in research and practice. *Educational Researcher, 31*(7), 3–14.

Ravitch, D. (Ed.). (1995a). *Debating the future of American education: Do we need national standards and assessment?* Washington, DC: Brookings Institution.

Ravitch, D. (1995b). *National standards in American education: A citizen's guide*. Washington, DC: Brookings Institution.

Rodd, J. (1999). Encouraging young children's critical and creative thinking skills. *Childhood Education, 75*, 350–353.

Roskos, K., & Christie, J. F. (2002). Knowing in the doing—observing literacy learning in play. *Young Children, 57*(2), 46–54.

Ross, M. E. (2000). Science their way. *Young Children, 55*(2), 6–10.

Russell, G. S. (1970). *The language experience approach to the teaching of reading*. New York: Harper Row.

Santos, R. M. (2004). Ensuring culturally and linguistically appropriate assessment of young children. *Young Children, 59*(1), 48–51.

Sawyer, R. (1953). *Journey cake, ho!* New York: Viking Press.

Schellenberg, E. G. (2003). Does exposure to music have beneficial side effects? In I. Peretz & R. Zatorre (Eds.), *The cognitive neuroscience of music*. New York: Oxford University Press.

Seefeldt, C. (1995). Art: A serious work. *Young Children, 50*(3), 39–45.

Seefeldt, C. (2005). *Social studies for the preschool/primary child* (7th ed). Upper Saddle River, NJ: Pearson.

Seefeldt, C. (in press). Science, art and music. *Early Childhood Today*.

Seefeldt, C., & Galper, A. (Eds.). (1998). *Continuing issues in early childhood education* (2nd Ed.). Upper Saddle River, NJ: Merrill.

Seefeldt, C., & Galper, A. (2000). *Active experiences for active children: Social studies*. Upper Saddle River, NJ: Merrill.

Seefeldt, C., & Galper, A. (2004). *Active experiences for active children: Math*. Upper Saddle River, NJ: Merrill.

Seefeldt, C., & Wasik, B. (2002). *Kindergarten: Fours and fives go to school*. Upper Saddle River, NJ: Merrill.

Segatti, L., Brown-DuPaul, J., & Keyes, T. L. (2003). Using everyday materials to promote problem solving in toddlers. *Young Children, 58*(5), 12–16.

Seo, K. (2003). What children's play tells us about teaching mathematics. *Young Children, 58*(1), 28–34.

Sendak, M. (1988). *Where the wild things are*. New York: Harper & Row. (Original work published 1963)

Simon, S., Fauteux, N., & Cushman, D. (2002). *Let's try it out on the playground*. New York: Simon & Schuster.

Spillane, J. P., Reiser, B. J., & Reimer, T. (2002). Policy implementation and cognition: Reframing and refocusing implementation research. *Review of Educational Research, 72*(3), 387–431.

Stevenson, R. L. (1923). *A child's garden of verses*. Chicago, IL: Albert Whitman.

Strickland, D. S., & Morrow, L. M. (2000). *Beginning reading and writing*. New York: Teachers College Press.

Tanner, D., & Tanner, L. (1990). *History of the school curriculum*. New York: Macmillan.

Taylor, B. M., & Pearson, P. D. (2003). *Effective schools and accomplished teachers: Lessons about primary-grade reading instruction in low-income schools*. Mahwah, NJ: Lawrence Erlbaum.

U.S. Department of Education (USED). (2004). *No child left behind*. [Web site]. Retrieved November 12, 2004, from http://www.ed.gov/nclb/landing.jhtml

U.S. Department of Health and Human Services (USHHS). (2000). *Head Start child outcomes framework*. Washington, DC: Author.

U.S. Department of Health and Human Services (USHHS). (2002). *Program performance standards for the operation of Head Start programs by grantee and delegate agencies*. Washington, DC: Author.

U.S. Department of Health and Human Services (USHHS). (2004). *Head Start reauthorization bill*. Washington, DC: Author.

Vacca, J. A., & Vacca, R. T. (2003). *Reading and learning to read*. New York: Allyn & Bacon.

VanFossen, P. J. (2003). Using literature circles to teach about immigration. *Social Studies and the Young Learner, 15*(4), 24–29.

Viorst, J. (1978). *Alexander, who used to be rich last Sunday*. New York: Atheneum.

Vygotsky, L. (1986). *Thought and language*. Cambridge, MA: MIT Press.

Wasik, B., Bond, M. A., & Hindman, A. (2001). Beyond the

pages of a book: Interactive book reading and language development in preschool classrooms. *Journal of Educational Psychology, 93,* 243–250.

Wells, R. (1997). *Bunny money.* New York: Dial Books for Young Readers.

Wheatly, K. L. (2003). Promoting the use of content standards: Recommendations for teacher educators. *Young Children, 58*(2), 96–102.

Whitehurst, G. J., & Longman, C. J. (1998). Child development and emergent literacy. *Child Development, 69,* 261–272.

Wilson, B. (1966). The development and testing of an instru-ment to measure aspective perception of paintings. (Doctoral dissertation, Ohio State University. 1966). *Dissertation Abstracts International, 27,* 2107A.

Wing, H. (1969). *What is big?* New York: Holt.

Winner, E., & Hetland, L. (2000). The arts and academic achievement: What the evidence shows. *Journal of Aesthetic Education, 34*(3–4), 300–306.

Wraga, W. G., & Hiebowitsh, P. S. (2003). Toward a renaissance in curriculum theory and development in the USA. *Journal of Curriculum Studies, 35,* 425–437.

Wylie, R. E., & Durrell, D. D. (1970). Teaching vowels through phonograms. *Elementary English, 47,* 787–791.

Index

About the Author

Carol Seefeldt (1935–2005) was a professor of human development at the Institute for Child Study, University of Maryland, College Park, for the past 30 years. She received the Distinguished Scholar-Teacher Award from the university and was also a visiting scholar at the Johns Hopkins University, Krieger School of Arts and Sciences. She published 32 books and over 150 scholarly research articles for teachers and parents. In addition, she edited special issues of journals, such as *Childhood Education* and the *Elementary School Journal*. Her recent books included *Kindergarten: Fours and Fives Go to School*, *Playing to Learn*, and the series *Active Experiences for Active Children*.

Dr. Seefeldt received her B.A. from the University of Wisconsin, her M.A. from the University of South Florida, and her Ph.D. from Florida State University, all in early childhood education. During her 40 years in the field, she taught at every level from 2-year-old nursery school through the third grade. She also worked extensively with graduate and undergraduate students at university level. In Florida she directed a church-related kindergarten and served as Regional Training Officer for Project Head Start. She also conducted training programs for Head Start teachers, teachers of migrant children, and teachers in Japan and Ukraine. Because of her expertise, she was a frequent guest on radio and television talk shows.

Dr. Seefeldt's research interests revolved around curriculum development and program evaluation as well as intergenerational attitudes. Her research on children's attitudes toward the elderly continues to be cited. She evaluated the Montgomery County Head Start–Public School Transition Demonstration, a comprehensive program similar to Head Start that follows former Head Start children and their families from Head Start through Grade 3.